J. O. Madick, O. Cincinnati

Beauty, Health and Complexion

J. O. Madick, O. Cincinnati

Beauty, Health and Complexion

ISBN/EAN: 9783337225698

Printed in Europe, USA, Canada, Australia, Japan

Cover: Foto ©Lupo / pixelio.de

More available books at **www.hansebooks.com**

BEAUTY, HEALTH and COMPLEXION

—OVER—

...IPTS, ...
...AND ...

J. O. MADICK & CO., FIFTH AND RACE
CINCINNATI, O.

SYRACUSE, N. Y., July 10, 1895.

GENTLEMEN:—I enclose you money order for fifty more books. Send at once. They sell like hot cakes. Respectfully, MRS. GEO. WELSH.

ST. LOUIS, Mo., July 14, 1895.

J. O. MADICK & Co., Cincinnati, O.

GENTLEMEN:—Received the twenty-five books, also pair of lace curtains as a premium. They are beauties. Will soon send you an order for fifty more books. Yours truly, MRS. JOHN BRANDT.

RACINE, WIS., Aug 4. 1895.

GENTLEMEN:—Would not be without your book if it cost $5.00. My little girl was cured of a severe case of Whooping Cough.
Yours truly, MRS. JOS. OKER.

XENIA, O., July 1, 1895.

MESSRS. J. O. MADICK & CO.

GENTLEMEN:—We no longer require a physician's services since buying one of your books. It has saved us quite a little money in doctor bills.
Gratefully yours, MRS. MALVINA WELLS.

PIQUA, O., Aug 16, 1895

GENTLEMEN:—Words can hardly express the thanks I owe you for your valuable book. My little boy was taken with a severe case of croup and I believe would have died but for you. Respectfully, MRS. CHAS. LAWRENCE.

PARKERSBURG, W. VA., July 14, 1895.

GENTLEMEN:—No person should be without your book. We cannot understand how we ever got along without it.
Yours truly, MRS. CHAS. PARKER.

IRONTON, O., June 29, 1895.

MESSRS. J. O. MADICK & CO., Cincinnati, O.

GENTLEMEN:—I enclose money order $7.50 for fifty books. Everybody speaks very highly of it and I expect to sell one thousand right in this town
Yours truly, MRS NORA HENRY

DENVER, COL., July 20, 1895.

GENTLEMEN:—My wife says she wouldn't be without your book for $50.00. By using one of the receipts she was cured of rheumatism of five years' standing. Respectfully, CHAS. A. PARKER

PITTSBURG, PA., July 3, 1895.

GENTLEMEN:—Please send me five more books for some relatives of mine. I recommend it very highly. Bought mine from one of your agents
MRS. CHAS. LICHTENSTEIN

QUINCY, ILL., Aug. 8, 1895.

GENTLEMEN:—I have used several receipts out of your book and find every one gives perfect satisfaction. Respectfully, MRS. HOWARD WHITE

CINCINNATI, O., June 29, 1895.

J. O MADICK & CO.

GENTLEMEN:—I do not understand how you can publish and sell such a good book for so little money. MILLIE MYERS, 110 Nassau St

CINCINNATI, O., July 10, 1895.

J. O. MADICK & Co., City.

I would not be without "Beauty, Health and Complexion" if it cost $10.
I am, MISS MINNIE RONSHEIM

BEAUTY,...
...HEALTH and...
COMPLEXION

COMPRISING MOST USEFUL RECEIPTS FOR

...kin, Beautifying the Complexion, Removing Freckles, S... Blemishes, Eradicating Superfluous Hair, Reliable F... Face Powders, Sachet Powders, Face Bleaches, Face... , Toilet Water, Hair Tonics, Bleaches, Hair Dyes, Po... Fluids, Perfumes, Colognes, Valuable Prescriptions fo... of Headache, Colds, Tonsilitis, Catarrh, Bronchitis, Indig... , Dyspepsia, Biliousness, Diarrhœa, Constipation, Spasm... ...arache, Toothache, Insomnia, Fevers, Diphtheria, Dropsy, Lumbago, and How to Care for the Teeth, Hair and Feet. Notes on the Care of Children and a Hundred Other Different Things.

...s been compiled by three of the most eminent ...d States and has taken over two solid years of ...

.....PRICE, 50 CENTS.....

PUBLISHED BY J. O. MADICK & CO.,
Fifth and Race,   CINCINNATI

Entered according to Act of Congress in the year 1895, by
J. O. MADICK & CO.,
In the office of the Librarian of Congress, at Washington, D. C.

Any infringment of any part upon any recipe, prescription or formula will be prosecuted to the fullest extent of the law.

PREFACE.

Good general health is an important factor towards beauty and loveliness, for beauty is a power in itself, which is well nigh irresistible. Women all recognize it and men bow in humble submission before its shrine.

Of course if nature has been lavish in her gifts, not much need be done; if, on the contrary, the skin, upon which so much of beauty depends, is ill favored or has been misused, a remedy must be called in as a help to nature.

A face not marred by scars or missing features, with the aid of the proper treatment, may be made positively beautiful.

Of course to be beautiful one must have perfect health, and one of the first things to be considered is the bath. Plenty of clear, soft water, soft towels and pure soap are accessories without which good health can not be secured. A warm bath is advised before retiring; this will induce refreshing sleep. And in the morning a thorough sponging with tepid water. Cold water is best on the face, as it gives firmness.

Be moderate in eating. Never overcrowd the stomach, and avoid all fatty foods and pastries. Take all the exercise possible.

By careful observance of the above and with the aid of the appropriate remedies for all ordinary ailments, found in this book, any person can have perfect health, thereby securing a beautiful face and form, which are so highly prized by all refined people.

CAUTION.

The dose given in every case are for an adult. Great care should be taken when these medicines are given to children ; the dose should be smaller to suit the age of the child. This matter can safely be left to the druggist who compounds the prescription. The age of the person should be written on the receipt. The best drugs and medicines should be used, or they will not have the desired effect, and the publishers be blamed for giving a poor receipt or prescription, when their desire has been to furnish the public with only those that are really valuable for the purposes named.

For Bust, Face and Complexion.

Developing the Bust.

At the morning and evening bath the breast should be lightly sponged with cold water containing one-half teaspoonful of powdered alum to the pint, then dried by gentle friction with a soft towel. This will stimulate the circulation and make the flesh firm. Should it be desirable to assist in greater development, *gentle* massage or manipulation may be given daily, using the bare hand with the following lotion :

Spirits camphor	½ drachm
Tincture myrrh	½ ounce
Alcohol	1 "
Peppermint water	2½ ounces—Mix.

If at first this feels too strong, add water.

After using this lotion with gentle manipulation the skin will glow and new life will be felt coursing through the parts. This, with the removal of pressure, will be followed in due time by a gratifying increase in size and firmness.

Freckles.

Glycerine	½ ounce
Lactic acid	½ "

Mix. To be applied night and morning with a sponge or soft rag.

Buttermilk for Freckles.

Fresh buttermilk is said to remove tan, freckles, sunburn, or moth spots; its chief advantage is its complete harmlessness. Bathe the face, neck and arms with a silk sponge or soft cloth dipped in fresh buttermilk before retiring, wiping off the surplus lightly. In the morning wash off with clear water, using a soft towel. This will banish freckles and tan, and keep the skin smooth and soft.

Freckle Lotion.

For removing freckles, discolorations of the skin, and to soften and whiten the face and hands.

Glycerine (best)	3	ounces
Oil of lemon	½	drachm
Rosewater	1	pint
Citric acid	⅙	ounce
Oil of sweet almonds	½	drachm

Rub acid in oils, gradually add glycerine, then rose water i divided portions until the whole is well mixed. Shake well befor using and apply freely night and morning.

Freckles.

Carbolic acid is said to be a certain cure for freckles. Th skin, first washed and dried, is stretched with two fingers of th left hand, and each freckle is carefully touched with a drop of pur carbolic acid, which is allowed to dry on the skin. Under its ac tion the part becomes white and burns for a few minutes. In fron eight to ten days the cauterized skin falls of, and the spot, at firs a rose red, assumes its natural color.

Freckles.

Muriate ammonia	4	parts
Dilute muriatic acid	5	"
Glycerine	30	"
Lait virginal	50	"

Mix. Touch the freckles twice daily with a small brusl dipped in the above.

Lait virginal is made as follows:

Tincture benzoin	1	part
Rose water	4	parts

Shake well.

Freckles and Liver Marks.

Corrosive sublimate	4	grains
Zinc sulphate	½	drachm
Alcohol	2	ounces

Mix. Apply morning and night.

Tan and Freckles.

Rose water	6	ounces
Glycerine	½	ounce
Bitter almond water	2½	drachms
Tincture benzoin	2½	"
Borax	1½	"

Rub the borax with the glycerine, gradually add the rose and almond water; lastly add the tincture benzoin, agitating constantly. Apply night and morning.

Freckle Wash.

Alcohol	10	fl. drachms
Orange flower water	5	"
Glycerine	10	"
Sulphocarbolate of zinc	1	drachm
Rose water, sufficient to make	12½	ounces

Mix and apply twice a day.

Freckle Lotion.

Angelica root	1¾	ounces
Black hellebore root	1¾	"
Storax	¾	ounce
Oil bergamot	2½	drachms
" citronella	2½	"
Alcohol	2	quarts

Macerate for a week and filter.

Freckles.

Corrosive sublimate	10	grains
Alcohol	2	ounces
Rose water	2	"

Mix. Apply morning and night.

Freckles.

Lactic acid	½	ounce
Glycerine	½	"

Freckles.

...sium .... 3 drachms
... . 2 "
...water .... 2 ounces
...make .... 8 "

...morning,

Moth Patches.

...ate .... 1 drachm
...bismuth .... 1 "
.... 1 ounce

...g to bed. Wash off in the morning with
...warm water and apply a little vaseline.

...dones, or Blackheads.

...althy condition of the skin. A concretion
... the pores of the skin, the surface becom-
...eric dust. Due attention to the proper
... essential to a cure. Constipation is most
...h an occasional dose of calomel (calomel,
...sodium 10 grains, in the morning, on an
...following mixture:

. ... 1½ drachms
... . 16 grains
...ic acid .... 2 ounces
. ... 8 "

...poonful in water before breakfast.

...out the contents of each blackhead every
... water, followed by:

...ur .... 1 drachm
...y (5 per cent.) ...... ½ "
.... 1 ounce

...t.

Acne.

.... ½ drachm
.... 1 ounce

...d morning.

Pimples (Acne).

Wash the affected parts with warm suds, rub well and frequently, in so doing express the contents of the pimples and apply the following mixture:

    Flowers sulphur............................25   grains
    Tincture camphor.........................1½ drachms
    Lime water....................................2½ ounces

Mix.

Acne, or Pimples.

    Tincture benzoin..........................1½ drachms
    Corrosive sublimate.....................4   grains
    Glycerine......................................2   ounces
    Water..2   "

Mix. Use locally.

Pimples.

    White precipitate.........................½ drachm
    Vaseline.......................................½ ounce
    Oil of roses..................................5 drops

Make an ointment. To be applied externally.

Pimples.

    Tannin..1½ drachm
    Flowers of sulphur......................2½ drachms
    Vaseline.......................................3   ounces

Mix. Apply to the part affected on going to bed.

Comedo.

When the blackheads are numerous and small, the following gives excellent results:

    Dilute ascetic acid.......................1 ounce
    Glycerine......................................2 ounces
    Kaolin...3 "

Mix. Apply at night.

Green soap, followed by a bland ointment, or cold cream, is often beneficial.

Where the blood is poor, patient pale, etc.:

> Pill carbonate iron ½ drachm
> Extract ignatia 2 grains
> Arsenious acid 1 grain

Make into 20 pills. Dose: one pill after meals.

Comedo.

When the blood is impure, especially in cases where there is a marked yellowish point to the "pimples:"

> Sublimed sulphur ½ ounce
> Carbonate magnesium 6 drachms

Mix, and divide into 12 powders. Dose: 1 to 2 powders in syrup, before breakfast.

Acne.

An application of corrosive sublimate in emulsions of almond oil (½ grain of the former to 1 ounce of the latter) has been highly recommended.

Acne.

> Liquor Potassae 1 drachm
> Rose water 1 ounce

Mix. Apply with sponge twice daily.

Lassar's Paste for Acne.

> Naphthol 2½ drachms
> Washed sulphur 1½ ounces
> Green soap 6 drachms
> Vaseline .6 "

Mix. This paste is to be left in place after application from one-half to one hour.

Stimulating Lotion for Blackheads.

> Tincture cantharides .4 drachms
> " capsicum 1 ounce
> Castor oil ½ drachm
> Glycerine, to make 4 ounces

Mix. Apply at night on retiring.

Blackheads.

Thymol..10 grains
Boric acid....................................2 drachms
Tincture witch hazel....................1 ounce
Rose water..................................4 ounces

Mix. Mop it well over the surface twice daily.

Blackheads.

Potassium carbonate ....3 drachms
Distilled water.............................3½ ounces
Oil cinnamon..............................2 drops
Oil rose.......................................1 drop

Mix. To be used with a sponge.

Especially serviceable where the skin is shiny from excessive oily secretion.

Sunburn.

Emulsion of almonds ....2 ounces
Corrosive sublimate ....1 grain

Mix. Apply to the affected part with a rag of soft material or a sponge.

Sunburn Lotion.

Powdered copperas, pure..........18 grains
Citric acid..................................1 drachm
Camphor, spirits.......................2 drachms
Elder flower water.....................3 ounces

Mix. Use as a wash twice a day.

Chapped Lips.

Compound tincture benzoin ......2 drachms
Glycerine....................................6 "

Mix. Apply 3 or 4 times a day with a camel's hair pencil.

Face Bleach.

Beta-naphthal............................5 grains
Glycerine....................................3 ounces
Cologne.....................................3 "

Face Bleach.

(Said to resemble Mme. Ruppert's)

Corrosive sublimate .... 8 grains
Tincture benzoin .... 1 drachm
Water sufficient to make .... 8 ounces

Mix. Apply night and morning.

Skin Gloss.

Carbonate potassium .... 1¼ ounces
Powdered spermaceti .... 1¼ "
Starch powder .... 1 pound
Gum benzoin .... ¾ ounce
Oil bitter almonds .... 2½ drachms

Preserve in well closed boxes. For use, stir some into water, and apply locally.

Skin Lotion.

Glycerine .... 4 ounces
Cologne water .... 2 "
Borax .... 2 "
Alcohol .... 2 "
Camphor water .... 20 "

Mix. To be used with a silk sponge night and morning.

Face Powder.

Finely powdered carbonate of magnesium .... ½ pound
Powdered talc .... 1 "
Oil rose .... 8 drops
Oil neroli .... 20 "
Extract jasmine .... ounce
Extract musk .... 1 drachm

Mix.

Face Powder.

Powdered talc .... 1 pound
Extract jasmine .... ¼ ounce
Oil rose .... 8 drops

Pass through No. 100 sieve.

Face Powder.

Prepared chalk	1 pound
Powdered orris root	2 drachms
Oil of roses	4 drops

Mix carefully. This is a delightful and perfectly harmless face powder.

Face Powder.

Corn starch	7 pounds
Rice flour	1 pound
Powdered talc	1 "
" orris root	1 "
Extract cassia	3 ounces
" jasmine	1 ounce

Mix.

Face Powder.

Powdered talc	1 ounce
" magnesium carbonate	1 "
Finest "crown" zinc white	1 "
Otto of rose (or oil of orris)	6 drops

Mix.

Cold Cream to Remove Wrinkles.

Lanolin	8 ounces
Vaseline	2 "
Rose water	2 grains
Vanillin	3 "
Oil rose	2 drops

Mix in mortar without heat.

If applied morning and night will remove wrinkles. Lanolin, one of the constituents in the above, is a true skin food. Wrinkles are caused by the absorption of adipose tissue. Lanolin being absorbed into the skin, gives nutriment to wasted tissue; hence, in time will cause eradication of wrinkles.

Cold Cream.

Oil of sweet almonds	8 ounces
White wax	2 "
Rose water	4 "
Powdered borax	1 drachm
Oil rose geranium	20 drops

Melt the wax and oil together with a gentle heat. Dissolve the borax in the rose water and heat to the boiling point, then mix with the wax and oil and stir constantly until cold.

Cold Cream to Remove Wrinkles.

Spermaceti	3 ounces
White wax	3 "
Nut oil	22 "
Alcohol	1 ounce
Water	4 ounces
Chloroform	10 drops
Oil rose geranium	30 "
Oil bergamot	6 "

Mix.

Cold Cream to Remove Wrinkles.

White wax	2 ounces
Spermaceti	3 "
Almond oil	8 "
Prepared lard	5 "
Water	6 "
Oil rose	10 drops
Oil bergamot	10 "

Mix.

Camphor Ice.

White vaseline	8 ounce
Hard paraffin	5 "
Camphor	2 "
Menthol crystals	10 grains

Heat vaseline and paraffin, when melted add camphor and menthol and stir till cool.

Cream Balm.

White wax	1 drachm
Paraffin	½ "
Oil sweet almonds	2 drachms

Melt over gentle heat, then add vaseline and stir well until cold. Having dissolved in a mortar ½ drachm soda nitrate in ½ drachm of water, mix the above salve thoroughly with this solution, and finally add, with constant stirring—

Oil lemon .... 10 drops
Oil orange .... 2 "

Glycerine Lotion.

For Chapped Hands, Lips, Sore Nipples and Rough Face.

Glycerine .... 6 ounces
Rose water .... 2 "
Zinc oxide .... 1 drachm
Tincture benzoin .... ½ "

Mix and shake well before using.

Glycerine Jelly.

Thin French gelatine .... ½ ounce
Water .... 5 ounces
Glycerine of borax .... 10 "
Triple rose water .... 6 "

Soak the gelatine in the water till soft, warm till dissolved, then incorporate the other ingredients.

Borax Lotion.

(Excellent to use after shaving.)

Powdered borax .... 1 drachm
Glycerine .... 1 ounce
Bay rum sufficient to make 4 ounces

Mix.

Glycerine Jelly—Carbolated.

Isinglass, French .... 1 ounce
Glycerine .... 16 ounces
Water .... 3 "
Carbolic acid .... 1 drachm

Mix.

Cold Cream of Roses.

Melt together 1 ounce each of white wax and spermaceti, adding 4 ounces oil of almonds, and gradually 4 fluid ounces best rose water. Then stir very thoroughly as the mixture cools, forming a nice uniform emulsion, which may be colored to suit.

Healing Balm.

For Chapped Hands, Lips and Face.

Glycerine, best .... 4 ounces
Rose water .... 4 "
Subnitrate of bismuth .... 10 grains

Shake well and apply several times a day.

Glycerine Jelly—Solid.

French gelatine .... 120 grains
Glycerine .... 1½ ounces
Water .... ½ ounce
Oil rose .... 1 drop

Mix.

Perfume for Vaseline Pomade.

Oil bergamot .... 40 drops
Oil rose .... 5 "
Oil cinnamon .... 5 "

The vaseline should first be melted, and when nearly cool enough to harden, the above should be added and thoroughly stirred.

Superfluous Hair.

Sulphide barium .... 10 parts
Starch .... 5 "
Oxide zinc .... 5 "

Stir this with a little water, sufficient to form a paste, which is to be spread upon the hairy surface. In the course of ten minutes the skin becomes dry, and after removal of the paste will be found smooth. The paste should not be used two days in succession.

Shaving Soap.

Melt together 8 pounds best tallow, 6 pounds lard, 2 pounds castor oil and saponify with 2 pounds soda lye and 2 pounds potash lye, each of 37° strength. Perfume the finished soap to suit.

Mentholated Cream.

This preparation is frequently used by barbers as a cooling and grateful application to the skin after shaving. It is made as follows: Put ½ ounce best gum tragacanth in 12 ounces water, and let stand with occasional shaking for two or three days ; then add 3 drachms glycerine and 40 grains menthol dissolved in ½ ounce alcohol. Color pink with tincture cudbear.

Digestion.

Average number of hours and minutes required for the digestion of various articles of food :

Apples, sweet [boiled]	2:30		Lamb [boiled]	2:30
Barley [boiled]	2:00		Milk [raw]	2:15
Beans, Lima [boiled]	2:30		Milk [boiled]	2:00
Beef [roasted]	3:00		Mutton [boiled]	3:00
Beef [fried]	4:00		Mutton [roast]	3:15
Beef, salt [boiled]	2:45		Oysters [roast]	3:15
Bread	3:30		Oysters [stewed]	3:30
Butter	3:30		Pigs' feet, soused [boiled]	1:00
Cheese	3:30		Potatoes [baked]	2:30
Chicken [fricasseed]	2:40		Pork, salt [stewed]	3:00
Custard [baked]	2:45		Pork [roast]	3:15
Duck [roasted]	4:00		Rice [boiled]	1:00
Eggs [raw]			Sago [boiled]	1:45
Eggs [soft boiled]	3:00		Soup [barley]	1:30
Eggs [hard boiled]	3:30		Soup [chicken, etc., average]	3:15
Eggs [fried]	3:30		Tripe, soused [boiled]	1:00
Fish	2:45		Turkey [roast]	2:20
Fowl [roast]	4:00		Veal [boiled]	4:00
Hashed meat and vegetables	2:30		Veal [fried]	4:30

Health Maxims.

Don't sleep in the draught.
Don't go to bed with cold feet.
Don't stand over hot air registers.
Don't neglect constipated bowels.
Don't try to cool too quickly after exercising.
Don't use your voice very much when very hoarse.
Don't sleep in a room without proper ventilation.
Don't sleep with insecure false teeth in your mouth.
Don't stuff a cold lest you be obliged to starve a fever.
Don't eat merely to save food and get your money's worth.
Don't try to get along without flannel underclothing in winter.
Don't sleep in the same undergarmet you wear during the day.

For the Toilet.

Cologne Water—Good and Cheap.

Oil of bergamot	½ ounce
Oil of lemon	½ "
Oil of lavender	2 drachms
Acetic ether	1 drachm
Alcohol	1 quart

Mix.

Cologne.

Essence bergamot	2 drachms
Essence lemon	1 drachm
Oil neroli	20 drops
Oil rosemary	6 "
Strong alcohol	1 pint
Orange flower water	1 ounce

Mix.

Cologne.

Oil cedrat	7 drachms
Oil orange peel	7 "
Oil neroli, best	6 "
Oil rosemary	3 "
Oil bergamot	3 "
Deodorized alcohol	1 gallon

Mix and let stand one week.

Cologne—Excellent and Cheap.

Oil bergamot	1 ounce, 2 drachms
Oil lemon	1 "
Oil orange	6 drachms
Oil cloves	1 drachm
Tincture orris root	4 ounces
Cologne spirits	1 gallon
Rose water	3 pints

Put oils and tincture orris root into the spirits. Agitate several times during the day. Let stand over night, then add the water. Shake well and filter. A pleasant and inexpensive cologne and improves greatly with age.

Cologne.

Oil lavender	1	drachm
Oil neroli	2	drachms
Oil lemon	1½	"
Oil bergamot	3	"
Oil rose	3	drops
Musk	2	grains
Gum benzoin	20	"
Alcohol	40	ounces.

Digest for two or three days, and add—

Powdered talcum	3	drachms
Orange flower water	2	ounces

Let the mixture stand 7 days, then filter.

Rose.

Rose flowers	250 parts
Oil rose geranium	1 part
Oil rose	1 "
Essence ambergris	10 parts
Essence musk	10 "

Mix.

Rose.

Powdered orris root	½	pound
Rose leaves	1½	pounds
Ground sandal wood	4	ounces
Patchouly leaves	2	"
Extract of civet	½	ounce
Oil of rose geranium	30	drops
Otto of rose	20	"

Break up the leaves, and mix the whole together. The oils and extracts should be mixed with the powders previously.

Sweet Briar Scent.

Oil lavender	40 drops
Oil bergamot	80 "
Oil lemon	80 "
Otto rose	8 "
Oil verbena	1 "
Essential oil almonds	1 "
Essence musk	120 "
Rectified spirit	1 ounce

Mix.

Lavender.

Lavender flowers	80 parts
Gum benzoin, powdered	20 "
Oil bergamot	1 part
Oil lavender, English	2 parts

Rub together.

Musk.

Grain musk	8 grains
Powdered orris root	8 ounces
Powdered ammonium carbonate	3 grains
Oil of rhodium	2 drops

Rub the musk with ammonium carbonate, and mix the whole together

Ess. Bouquet.

Powdered orris root	½ pound
Musk	5 grains
Otto of rose	½ drachm
Essence of lemon	15 drops
Essence of bergamot	1 drachm

Mix.

Violet.

Powdered cassia buds	¼ pound
Powdered black currant leaves	¼ "
Powdered orris root	½ "
Rose leaves	¼ "
Essential oil bitter almonds	6 drops
Musk	15 grains
Gum benzoin in powder	6 drachms

Mix.

Jockey Club.

Powdered orris root	4	ounces
Powdered sandal wood	5½	drachms
Extract of musk	1½	"
Extract of civet	50	grains
Oil of bergamot	50	drops
Oil of rose	4	"

Mix well together.

Heliotrope.

Coarsely powdered orris root	4	ounces
Vanilla beans, powdered	1½	drachms
Musk	2	grains
Essential oil bitter almonds	8	drops
Otto of rose	8	"

Mix.

Heliotrope.

Powdered orris root	4	ounces
Ground red rose petals	2	"
Ground tonka beans	1	ounce
Ground vanilla beans	½	"
Grain musk	15	grains
* Essence bitter almonds	50	drops

*Made by adding 8 drops essential oil bitter almonds to one ounce alcohol.

Lavender Water.

Grape spirit	1 pint
Oil lavender	1 ounce
Extract ambergris	2 ounces

Mix and filter.

Toilet Vinegar.

Essence bergamot	20	drops
Essence ambergris	4	drachms
Essence vanilla	30	drops
Oil neroli	30	"
Acetic acid, strong	160	"
Alcohol	6	ounces

Mix.

Florida Water.

Oil lavender	2 drachms
Oil bergamot	2 "
Oil lemon	2 '
Oil neroli	1 drachm
Oil melissa	30 drops
Oil rose	10 "
Tincture turmeric	1 drachm
Alcohol	1 quart

Mix.

Aromatic Vinegar.

Concentrated acetic acid	8 ounces
Oil English lavender	2 drachms
Oil English rosemary	1 drachm
Oil cloves	1 "
Camphor	1 ounce

First dissolve the bruised camphor in the acetic acid, then add the perfumes; after remaining together for a few days, with occasionally shaking, it is to be strained, and is then ready for use.

Toilet Water.

Oil lavender flowers	2 drachms
Oil lemon	2 "
Tincture of turmeric	1 drachm
Oil neroli	1 "
Oil balm	30 drops
Oil rose	10 "
Strong alcohol	1 quart
Dilute alcohol	1 "

Mix the oils with the strong alcohol, then with the dilute alcohol. The finished product will mix with water and make a fine toilet water.

Fumigating Pastilles.

Oil nutmeg	1 drachm
Oil cloves	1 "
Oil cinnamon	½ "
Powdered saltpeter	½ ounce
Powdered charcoal	½ pound

Mucilage, enough to make a thick paste. Shape into small cones. To use, touch a cone with a lighted match.

Fumigating Pastilles.

Powdered gum benzoin	1	ounce
Powdered cascarilla bark	1	"
Powdered myrrh	2½	drachms

Smelling Salts.

Muriate of ammonia	3½	ounces
Salts of tartar	4½	"
Oil of lavender	½	ounce
Oil of bergamot	1	drachm
Oil of cloves	16	drops
Oil of lemon	3	drachms

Strong water of ammonia enough to moisten.

Glycerine Cream.

Glycerine	6	ounces
Boric acid	½	ounce

Dissolve by heat; then add the following, previously mixed:

Tincture arnica	½	ounce
Rose water	5	ounces

Antiseptic Dusting Powder for Tourists.

Violet powder	8	ounces
Boric acid, powdered	4	"
Sylicylic acid	1	ounce
Eucalyptus oil to perfume.		

Mix thoroughly.

Incense.

Frankincense	3	ounces
Benzoin gum, powdered	3	"
Amber, powdered	3	"
Lavender flowers	1	ounce

This is intended to be lighted upon coals, a stove, or hot shovel, to diffuse a pleasant aroma in an apartment, and to destroy noxious effluvia. By adding powdered saltpeter 1½ ounces to this mixture, an aromatic pastile powder will result, which will burn of itself on touching with a lighted match.

Spanish Paste.

For perfuming jewelry boxes, glove or handkerchief boxes, fine leather goods, shoes, belts, etc.

Powdered ambergris	¾ ounce
Powdered gum benzoin	1½ "
Powdered musk	¼ "
Powdered vanilla bean	¼ "
Powdered orris root	¾ "
Powdered cinnamon bark	¼ "
Oil bergamot	1½ "
Oil rose	¼ "
Gum arabic	1½ "
Glycerine	1½ "

Add water drop by drop until a doughy mass is formed. Divide into pieces the size of a filbert.

For the Teeth.

Tooth Powder.

Precipitated chalk	1 ounce
Phosphate calcium	1 "
Powdered orris root	2 drachms

Mix.

Tooth Powder.

Chlorate of potassium	15 grains
Prepared chalk	30 "
Powdered guaiacum	10 "
Carbonate of magnesia, powdered	½ ounce
Attar of roses	½ drop
Boric acid, powdered	20 grains

Mix together thoroughly. Will polish enamel of teeth, take off tartar and sweeten breath. Nothing better for the teeth.

Tooth Powder.

Powdered cuttle fish bone	1 ounce
Powdered chew stick	1 "
Powdered soap	½ "
Powdered orris root	3 ounces
Precipitated chalk	12 "

Flavor with oil of wintergreen and color with carmine to suit.

Toothache.

Alcohol	4 drachms
Camphor	2 "
Menthol crystals	1 drachm
Oil of eucalyptus	30 drops
Oil of cloves	10 drops

Moisten a small pledget of cotton and insert in the cavity of an aching tooth or on the adjacent gum.

Toothache.

Morphine sulphate	4 grains
Atropine	1 grain
Water	1 ounce

Mix. A few drops on cotton placed in the cavity.

Toothache.

Laudanum	1 drachm
Acetate of lead	10 grains
Distilled water	½ drachm

Mix. Saturate a piece of absorbent cotton and place in the cavity of the tooth.

Tooth Wash.

Cloves	½ drachm
Cinnamon	½ "
Anise, coarsely powdered	½ "
Cochineal	20 grains
Alcohol	4 ounces

Macerate for one week, filter, and in the filtrate dissolve 5 drops oil peppermint.

Toothache.

Oil cloves	½ drachm
Oil peppermint	½ "

Mix. Moisten a small piece of cotton in this mixture and insert in the hollow tooth.

Liquid Dentrifice.

Powdered castile soap	1	ounce
Water	20	ounces

Dissolve and add

Oil cloves	½	drachm
Oil cinnamon	½	"
Oil nutmeg	15	drops
Powdered borax	6	drachms
Simple syrup	5	ounces
Solution burnt sugar	15	drops
Mix. Honey water	5	ounces

Camphorated Chalk.

Precipitated chalk	1	pound
Powdered orris root	½	"
Powdered camphor	¼	"

Powder the camphor by aid of chloroform or alcohol. Then sift the whole well together.

For Preserving the Teeth.

Use a teaspoonful of the following wash in a glassful of warm water:

Tannic acid	15	grains
Tincture iodine	8	drops
Tincture myrrh	8	"
Iodide potassium	12	grains
Mix. Rose water	4½	ounces

Gargle for Offensive Breath.

Salicylic acid	1 drachm
Bicarbonate soda	1 "
Saccharine	1 "
Alcohol	4 ounces

A teaspoonful in a cup of water, used as a gargle several times a day.

For the Hair.

Dandruff.

Local treatment is always necessary. If the scales are adherent they should be first removed by soaking in oil, after which apply—

> Alcohol .... ½ ounce
> Green soap .... 4 ounces

Mix.

Take a teaspoonful of this mixture with water and shampoo the part thoroughly. Then apply the following salve:

> Precipitated sulphur .... 2 drachms
> Cold cream .... 1 ounce
> Zinc oxide .... ½ drachm

Mix.

Dandruff.

> Chloral .... 1½ ounces
> Fluid extract jaborandi .... ½ ounce
> Glycerine .... 1¼ ounces
> Oil rose geranium .... 10 drops
> Oil lemon .... 2 "
> Water to make 2 pints.

Mix. Rub well into the roots of the hair about 3 times a week.

Dandruff.

> Best castor oil .... 2¼ ounces
> Cologne spirits, strongest ..... 1 pint

Mix. Rub gently on the scalp and use also as a dressing.

Lice.

> Carbolic acid .... 1 ounce
> Rose water .... ½ pint

Mix well. Rub in well with a stiff brush before going to bed.

Shampooing Powder.

Powdered borax	1 ounce
Powdered sal soda	1 "
Camphor	20 grains
Oil rosemary	10 drops

To be dissolved in a quart of water.

Shampooing Liquid.

Carbonate of Ammonia	½ ounce
Sal tartar	1 "
Water	1 pint
Tr. Cantharides	1 ounce
Bay Rum	1 pint

For Shampooing.

Aqua ammonia	4 ounces
Alcohol	32 "
Glycerine	2 "
Water	64 "

Mix thoroughly; add such perfume as desired. Can be prepared at home at trifling cost, and is a luxury as a scalp wash, cleaning the hair, etc.

Hair Tonic.

Fluid extract jarborandi	½ ounce
Quinine sulphate	10 grains
Glycerine	1 ounce
Cologne	2 ounces
Bay rum	2 "
Rose water	10 "

Mix.

Hair Tonic.

Castor oil	1 ounce
Oil bergamot	40 drops
Glycerine	3½ ounces
Tincture cantharides	4 drachms
Ammonia water	4 "
Alcohol to make	1 pint

Dissolve the oils in the alcohol, add the tincture, and gradually add the ammonia mixed with the glycerine.

Hair Tonic.

Cologne	2 ounces
Quinine sulphate	15 grains
Tincture cantharides	2 drachms
Borax	1 drachm
Ammonia water	1 "
Glycerine	3 ounces
Bay rum to make	1 pint

Mix and filter.

Quinine Hair Tonic.

Quinine	20 grains
Glycerine	1 ounce
Cologne	2 ounces
Fluid extract jaborandi	½ ounce
Water to make	½ pint

Mix. Rub well into the roots of the hair three or four times a week.

Hair Tonic.

Cologne spirits	4 ounces
Tincture of cantharides	2 "
Oil of lavender	10 drops
Oil of cloves	1 drop

Rub well into the scalp twice a week.

To Arrest Falling Out of Hair.

Gallic acid	45 grains
Olive oil	6 drachms
Vaseline	1½ ounces
Essence lavender	15 drops

Mix. This ointment is to be applied with friction to the part affected, morning and night, for the arrest of the disease.

Falling of Hair.

Fluid extract jaborandi	1½ ounces
Tincture cantharides	1½ drachms
Glycerine	1 ounce
Vaseline oil	1 "

Mix. Apply locally with a sponge at night.

Baldness.

Apply to the scalp a strong lather of coal tar soap, which should be removed after ten minutes, by tepid water, cooling gradually. After drying, shampoo with a little of the following:

Corrosive sublimate	10 grains
Glycerine	2 ounces
Alcohol	2 "
Water	5 "

Then apply a little strong alcohol, to which ½ per cent. of naphthol has been added. Finally, rub a little of this solution into the skin:

Salicylic acid	½ drachm
Tincture benzoin	1 "
Olive oil	3 ounces

Baldness.

Glycerine	1 ounce
Tincture Spanish Flies	1 drachm
Wool Fat	1 "
Quinine	20 grains
Spirits of nutmeg	2 ounces
Fluid extract of jaborandi	½ drachm
Rose water	1 pint

Mix. Apply every two or three days with a stiff brush. Shake well before using.

Baldness.

Tincture benzoin	2 drachms
Spirits chloroform	1 ounce
Ethereal tincture capsicum	5 drops
Tincture nux vomica	2 drachms
Alcohol	2½ ounces

Mix. Use locally night and morning.

Hair Restorer.

Quinine sulphate	20 grains
Powdered borax	½ drachm
Ammonia water	2 drachms
Tincture cinchona compound	½ ounce
Imported bay rum, to make	4 ounces

To one ounce of bay rum add the quinine and borax, add another ounce of bay rum, gradually add the ammonia, then sufficient bay rum to make 4 ounces, and filter.

Hair Invigorator.

Carbonate ammonia	4 drachms
Tincture cantharides	1 ounce
Castor oil	1 "
Alcohol	1 pint
Bay rum	2 pints

Mix. This compound will promote the growth of the hair and prevent it from falling out.

To Stimulate the Growth of Beard.

Aromatic spirits of ammonia	1 drachm
Cologne	2 ounces
Tincture cantharides	2 drachms
Oil rosemary	10 drops
Oil lavender	10 "

Mix. Apply to the face daily and await results.

Hair Curling Liquid.

Gum arabic	1 drachm
Sugar	1 "
Rose water	2 ounces

Mix and dissolve. Moisten the hair with the solution at bedtime; put the hair up in curl papers.

Hair Curling Liquid.

Borax	3 ounces
Gum arabic	1 drachm
Hot water	2 pints
Spirits of camphor	1½ fl. ounces

Dissolve the borax and the gum in hot water, and when nearly cold add the spirits camphor. On retiring at night wet the hair with this liquid.

Hair Bleach.

First shampoo the hair thoroughly with one ounce salts of tartar dissolved in one pint of water. Wash out well with water and dry hair with towels, then apply:

Peroxide hydrogen (10 vols.) .... 4 ounces

Apply with soft brush or sponge on retiring.

Hair Curling Liquid.

Salts tartar .... 2 drachms
Water of ammonia .... 1 drachm
Glycerine .... 4 drachms
Alcohol 12   "
Rose water .... 18 fl. ounces

Mix together. Moisten the hair, adjust it loosely, and it curls upon drying.

Lotion for Eyebrows:

Common salt .... 1 drachm
Chloride of ammonium .... 10 grains
Camphor 5   "
Oil of rosemary .... 10 drops
Alcohol .... 1 drachm
Water sufficient to make 1 ounce.

Dissolve the oil and camphor in the spirit, the salts in the water, and mix.

Stimulant Hair Dressing.

Tincture cayenne pepper .... ½ ounce
Cologne water .... 2½ ounces

Mix. Apply night and morning.

Dressing for the Hair.

Castor oil .... 12 ounces
Alcohol 2   "
Any handkerchief perfume 2   "
Solution carmine, sufficient to color.

To stimulate the growth of hair, add to the above

Sulphate of quinine .... 20 grains
Tincture of capsicum .... 15 drops
Tincture of cantharides 6   "

To Curl the Hair.

Steep ¾ ounces gum tragacanth for 48 hours in one pint rose water, stirring frequently; strain through a cloth, and let stand for a few days, then strain and work into it 8 drops of rose.

Hair Oil.

Oil bergamot	2 drachms
Oil cassia	15 drops
Oil bitter almonds	5 "
Benne oil	1 pint

Mix.

Cosmetic or Stick Pomade.

Melt ½ pound oil soap and ½ pound gum arabic in one pint rose water, adding one pound white wax, stirring constantly. When of proper consistency, add one ounce oil bergamot, and ½ drachm oil of thyme. This produces a fine white cosmetic. If a brown tint be desired, use burnt umber ground in oil. to be obtained of dealers in artists' supplies. For black, use ivory black, in oil.

For the Skin.

Scurvy.

Muriated tincture iron	2 drachms
Tincture cayenne pepper	10 drops
Quinine	30 grains
Distilled water to make 4 ounces.	

Mix. Take a teaspoonful three times a day before meals.

Odor from Perspiration.

For the unpleasant odor produced by perspiration, a source of vexation to many persons, place from one to two tablespoonfuls of compound spirits of ammonia in a basin of water. Washing the face, hands and arms with this leaves the skin as clean, neat and fresh as one could wish.

Acute Eczema.

Zinc carbonate	1 drachm
Lead	1 "
Sublimed sulphur	1 "
Powdered arrowroot	1 "

Mix. Use locally.

Acute Eczema.

Lead carbonate ... 4 drachms
Powdered starch ... 3 "
Lycopodium ... 4 "

Mix. Use locally.

Chronic Eczema.

Creosote ... 10 drops
Carbonate lead ... 2 drachms
Subnitrate bismuth ... 1 drachm
Calomel ... 10 grains
Olive oil ... 5 ounces

Mix. Use locally.

Eczema of the Breast.

Boric acid ... 1 drachm
Sublimed sulphur ... 10 grains
Ointment oxide zinc ... 1 ounce

Mix. Use locally.

Ointment for Scaly Eczema of the Scalp.

Salicylic acid ... 20 grains
Precipitated sulphur ... 1 drachm
Vaseline ... 1 ounce
Oil rose sufficient to perfume.

Mix thoroughly.

This ointment has a wide range of application, especially in scaly diseases of the scalp resulting in dandruff.

Eczema.

Zinc oxide ... 1 ounce
Glycerine ... 2 ounces
Mucilage gum arabic ... 2 "

Mix. Use locally.

In extensive patches of eczema this paste is very agreeable. If there be severe itching, one per cent. of carbolic acid may be added.

Eczema (Not Chronic).

Thymol .... 3 drachms
Oxide zinc .... 6½ "
Starch .... 6½ "
Lanolin .... 1½ ounces

Mix. Use as a salve.

Tetter.

White precipitate .... ½ drachm
Vaseline (carbolized) .... 1 ounce

For external use as directed by a physician.

Tetter.

Chloride of zinc .... 2 drachms
Glycerine .... 2 ounces

Mix. Rub on hands after washing.

Barber's Itch.

Vaseline .... 1 ounce
Flowers of sulphur .... 1 to 2 drachms
Oil of roses .... 5 drops

Mix. Use as a local application.

Itch.

Balsam Peru .... 1 ounce
Flowers of sulphur .... 2 drachms
Vaseline .... 3 ounces

Mix. Rub thoroughly over the body twice a day. Take a warm bath every three days at night.

Itch.

Oil of cade .... ½ drachm
Prepared lard .... 1 "

Mix. Use at night and in the morning.

Itch (Scabies).

Creolin .... 1 part
Peruvian balsam .... 20 parts

Mix, and apply locally.

Ointment for Itch.

Oil cade	3 drachms
Sublimed sulphur	4 "
Green soap	1 ounce
Lard	2 ounces

Mix. Apply locally morning and night.

Lotion for Itch.

Corrosive sublimate	4 grains
Alcohol	6 drachms
Ammonium chloride	½ drachm
Water sufficient to make 6 ounces.	

Use as a lotion.

Ointment for Itch.

Storax	2 drachms
Sulphur ointment	2 "
Vaseline sufficient to make 1 ounce.	

Apply after washing.

Salve for Itch (Scabies).

Lard	3½ ounces
Soft soap	1½ "
Naphthol	½ ounce
Powdered chalk	2½ drachms

Mix into a salve.

The treatment should not necessarily extend over 24 hours. If there is much itching, reduce the amount of naphthol, and if eczema, reduce the amount still further, as in such case the naphthol may produce considerable irritation.

For Ordinary Itching.

Morphine sulphate	6 grains
Powdered borax	4 drachms
Camphor water	6 ounces

Mix. Wash the parts first with castile soap and warm water and apply the above twice a day.

Itching.

Chloral hydrate	3 parts
Alcohol	20 "
Water	30 "

Mix, and use locally.

Persistent Itching.

Carbolic acid crystals	2 parts
Alcohol	10 "
Glycerine	20 "
Water	200 "

Mix, and use locally.

Troublesome Itching.

Cocaine alkaloid	20 grains
Lanolin	1 ounce

Mix. Use locally. This salve is especially useful for persistent itching on mucous surfaces.

Persistent Itching.

Gum camphor	1 drachm
Chloral hydrate	1 "
Cold cream	1 ounce

Mix. Use locally.

Chafe (Intertrigo).

Common to children, stout persons, and those having a delicate, sensitive skin. It occurs at such portions of the body where adjacent folds of skin rub together. Care in the selection of proper underwear, cleanliness and the judicious use of dusting powders are among the successful remedial measures. A good dusting powder is the following:

Powdered oxide zinc	1 ounce
Powdered prepared chalk	1 "
Powdered talc	2 ounces
Bicarbonate sodium	2 "

Mix. Use two or three times daily, after washing in cold water.

If the chafed surface has become raw from continued irritation and throws off a slimy, sticky discharge, the parts should be well cleansed, then touched over with a sponge dipped in a weak solution of "black wash." An application should then be made of the following soothing salve, which should be covered with a soft linen cloth:

    Oxide zinc _____ ½ drachm
    Powdered camphor_____40 grains
    Cold cream_____ 1 ounce
Mix.

Erysipelas.

    Glycerine _____ ½ ounce
    Muriated tincture of iron_____3 drachms
    Water enough to make_____2 ounces
Mix. Take a teaspoonful every three hours.

Erysipelas.

    Bromide of potassium_____2 drachms
    Chloral _____1 drachm
    Simple syrup _____1 ounce
    Water to make_____4 ounces
Mix. A tablespoonful every two to four hours, as may be necessary.

For Burns, Erysipelas and Fissure in Nipples.

    Glycerite of yolk of egg_____2 ounces
Paint the parts with a camel's hair brush.

Erysipelas.

    Tincture chloride iron _____2 drachms
    Glycerine _____2 "
Mix. Dose: Teaspoonful, well diluted in water, every two or three hours

Erysipelas.

    Tannic acid _____1 drachm
    Gum camphor_____2½ drachms
    Sulphuric ether_____2 ounces

Mix. Apply with camel's hair pencil over affected area every 3 or 4 hours, until a white, impervious coat is formed. Internally, give 10 drops tincture chloride of iron in ¼ glass water every hour the first day, every 2 hours the second day, every 3 hours the third day, and then 3 times daily after that until cured.

Hives.

A dose of salts, repeated as needed, and a local application to allay the itching, is all the treatment necessary. A sponge bath morning and night with water containing a little salt with ½ teaspoonful of spirits of camphor to the basin, is beneficial. To allay itching, the following should be applied:

Chloral hydrate 2	drachms
Morphine sulphate 10	grains
Peppermint water 4	ounces
Camphor water 4	"

Mix. For external use.

Citrate potassium .... ½	ounce
Bicarbonate sodium 3	drachms
Peppermint water 4	ounces

Mix. Dose: Teaspoonful every 2 or 3 hours.

For Intolerable Hives.

Chloral hydrate 2	drachms
Boric acid 3	"
Water 12	ounces

Mix. Apply to the itching skin.

Hives.

Carbolic acid 1	drachm
Alcohol 4	ounces
Water 1	pint

Mix. Apply locally night and morning, to quiet itching.

Hives.

Menthol 1	drachm
Olive oil 4	ounces

Mix. Use locally to allay irritation and itching.

Hives.

Vinegar 2 parts, water 1 part, used as a lotion will afford quick relief in the itching of hives or urticaria. Some recommend a lotion compound of baking soda dissolved in water.

To Remove Warts.

Calomel	1	drachm
Boric acid	½	"
Salicylic acid	10	grains

Mix and apply three times a day.

Warts.

Fuming nitric acid applied once a day with the burnt end of a match will destroy warts in a few days.

(See also Corn Remedies.)

Abcess or "Gathering."

Carbolic acid	8 grains
Water	1 ounce

Mix. Inject 10 drops into swelling and repeat every three days.

Abcess or "Gathering."

Hypophosphite sodium	80	grains
Hypophosphite calcium	160	"
Simple syrup	1½	ounces
Fennel water to make	4	"

Mix. Dose: 2 teaspoonfuls 4 times a day.

To Abort a Boil.

The early application of ointment of nitrate of mercury will frequently abort a boil.

Also oil of turpentine frequently applied.

Cure for Frostbite.

Purified chloroform	½	ounce
Tincture opium	½	"
Tincture aconite	½	"
Alcohol	½	"

Mix. Use locally as needed.

Chilblains.

Camphor	2 drachms
Cantharides	2 "
Table mustard	4 "
Oil cajuput	1 drachm
Oil rosemary	3 drachms
Alkanet	2 "
Oil turpentine	10 "

Macerate 10 days, frequently shaking, then filter.

Cure for Frostbite.

Tincture witch hazel	2 ounces
Tincture opium	2 "
Solution subacetate lead	2 "
Water	½ pint

Mix. Use locally.

Frostbite.

White wax	2 drachms
Spermaceti	2 "
Balsam Peru	1 drachm
Muriatic acid	2 drachms
Olive oil	3 ounces
Water	6 "

Make into a plaster and apply.

To Remove Tattooing.

Dr. Variot's method is as follows: Tattoo the skin in the usual way with a concentrated solution of tannin, following the original design. Then apply a crayon of nitrate of silver until the part tattooed with tannin blackens. Wipe off excess of moisture and allow matters to take their own course. Slight pain continues for two to four days, and after two months the scar which results will almost disappear.

To Prevent Pitting in Smallpox.

The entire head and face (except the eyes) and the neck, are covered with plaster consisting of carbolic acid 1 part and 15 parts each olive oil and starch. The body is covered over with a mixture of 3 parts salicylic acid, 30 parts starch and 70 parts olive oil.

Ringworm.

    Iodide potassium 8   grains
    Tincture of iodine................ ½ drachm
    Distilled water to make 1   ounce

Mix. With the finger rub in well spirits turpentine on the diseased surface and around it. Wash off in three or four minutes with hot water and carbolic soap and paint with a camel's hair pencil.

Ringworm.

    Corrosive sublimate.. ....2 grains
    Compound tincture benzoin..........1 ounce

Mix. Apply once a day. A few applications will suffice.

Flea Lotion.

    Soap bark, coarsely powdered........1 ounce
    Boiling water......................2 pints

Steep for an hour, strain and add:

    Corrosive sublimate... .... ½ ounce
    Muriatic acid   .... ½   "
    Turpentine.........................5   ounces
    Spirit of tar......................5   "

Shake well together, label "Poison," and use as follows:

To prevent the flea from striking, and for maggots—Mix 2 tablespoonfuls with a wine bottle of cold water.

To kill lice—Mix 3 tablespoonfuls with a wine bottle of cold water and rub on with a brush.

For mange—Mix 4 tablespoonfuls with a wine bottle of cold water, and rub the mixture in well with a brush every day until cured.

For Poisoning by Poison Ivy.

Make a strong tea of sassafras root; when cold, wet cloths in it and apply frequently to the parts affected. A day's treatment will usually effect a cure.

Ivy Poisoning.

Aristol freely dusted on will afford prompt relief in ivy poisoning.

The free use of lime water is also good.

For Stings from Poisonous Weeds, Etc.

Morphine ... 10 grains
Powdered borax ... 2 drachms
Carbolic acid (crystals) ... 1 drachm
Powdered gum arabic ... 4 drachms
Water to make half pint.

Mix. Shake thoroughly till a solution is made. Paint the part affected with a camel's hair brush or soft rag.

Bee Stings.

Aqua ammonia is a specific or sure cure for bee stings; it should be applied to the injured parts at once and thoroughly, when all pain and swelling will immediately subside.

For the Hands.

Treatment of Fissured Hands.

Wash the hands in lukewarm water, apply to the fissures or cracks a small quantity of the following:

Tannin ... 15 grains
Glycerine ... 5 drachms
Water ... 3½ ounces

After which the hands are allowed to dry. On retiring the following salve should be applied:

Extract of Rhatany ... 30 grains
Lanolin ... 1¾ ounces
Oil rose ... 2 drops

Gloves should be worn at night.

Eczema of the Hand.

Salicylic acid ... 25 grains
Starch powder ... 2 drachms
Powdered zinc oxide ... 2 "
Vaseline ... ½ ounce

Mix. Use twice daily.

For Red Hands.

Lanolin	10 ounces
Vaseline oil	3 "
Vanillin	1 grain
Otto of rose	5 drops

Mix. Apply at night on retiring.

Glycerine Jelly for the Hands.

Gum tragacanth	60 grains
Glycerine	2 ounces
Water	4 "
Extract rose	8 drops

Mix.

Glycerine Jelly for the Hands.

Gelatine	2 drachms
Glucose	1 ounce
Glycerine	6 ounces
Water	3 "
Oil rose	5 drops

Mix.

Chapped Hands.

Menthol	30 grains
Salol	40 "
Olive oil	40 "
Lanolin	4 ounces

This is especially serviceable where the hands are badly chapped.

Application for Chapped Hands.

Corn starch	2	parts
Glycerine	8	"
Perfume	1	part
Water	50	parts

Mix. Use as often as convenient after washing.

Chapped Hands.

Soft soap	64 parts
Spermaceti	16 "
Olive oil	4 "
Camphor	1 part
Alcohol	2 parts
Spirits of lemon	1 part
Water	64 parts

Mix. Apply on retiring.

Nail Powder.

Oxide tin, very fine	4 pounds
Carmine	¾ ounce
Oil bergamot	2½ drachms
Oil lavender	2½ "

Mix.

Nail Polish.

Pure oxide tin	1 ounce
Oil lavender flowers	30 drops
Carmine, sufficient to color.	

Rub on nail with finger or nail polisher.

Polish for Finger Nails.

Peroxide tin (putty powder)	5 ounces
Powdered gum tragacanth	6 grains
Glycerine	4 drachms

Rose water sufficient to make a paste. Color with ammonical solution of carmine.

For Felon or Whitlow.

Tincture of columbo	1 drachm
Dilute hydrochloric acid	2 drachms
Quinine	30 grains
Fluid extract nux vomica	½ drachm
Simple syrup enough to make 4 ounces.	

Mix. Dose: A teaspoonful 3 times a day, before meals.

For the Feet.

Care of the Feet.

Corns are the result of pressure. After the corn has been removed, find out where the shoe pinches then bathe the feet in cold water every morning upon arising and rub the part with prepared chalk.

For dry feet bathe in ice cold water.

For moist feet, inclined to perspire freely, use water as hot as you can stand it and bathe before going to bed.

If the feet swell after much walking put a little vinegar in the hot water. If they ache use a few drops of ammonia or a little borax. Rest the feet often by changing the shoes as frequently as possible.

For Corns and Bunions.

Salicylic acid .... 10 grains
Lard (free from salt) .... 7 drachms

Mix. Spread enough to cover the corn on a piece of patent lint; bind on with rubber adhesive plaster. Do this for two nights, then wash in quite warm water and remove the dead tissue with the finger nails. Avoid cutting corns at all times; it makes them worse.

For Soft Corns.

Oxide of zinc (Hubbucks) .... 10 grains
Morphine .... 1 grain

Mix. Sprinkle some of the powder on the corn and bind on with rubber adhesive plaster.

Corns and Warts.

Salicylic acid .... 1 drachm
Lactic acid .... 1 "
Collodion .... 10 drachms

Mix. This is recommended as an excellent application to corns and warts, effecting their removal in a short time.

Corns.

Pare the corn as deeply as possible, then apply the following every night for a week:

  Salicylic acid............................ 1 drachm
  Extract cannabis indica............... 10 grains
  Collodion .... 1 ounce

At the end of that time soak the feet in warm water and the corn will come off. In very obstinate cases a repetition of this procedure will be necessary.

Bunions.

  Compound tincture of iodine......... ½ ounce
  Iodide of Potassium..................... 5 grains

Mix. Apply to bunion with a camel's hair pencil.

Bunions.

  Tincture iodine........................... 1 drachm
  Tincture belladonna................... 1 "

Mix. Apply twice daily.

Perspiration Powder.

  Carbolic acid............................. 1 part
  Burnt alum................................ 4 parts
  Starch powder........................... 200 "
  French chalk............................. 4 "
  Oil of lemon............................. 2 "

Make a fine powder, to be applied to the hands and feet, or to be sprinkled inside of gloves or stockings.

Lotion for Offensive Feet.

  Burt alum................................. 30 grains
  Boracic acid............................. 30 "
  Rose water.............................. 1 ounce

Apply with soft sponge without rubbing just as shoes and stockings are removed, while the feet are yet moist. This is quite necessary, as also the care not to rub. Let this be repeated every two or three days in the evening.

Offensive Feet.

Beta naphthol	½ drachm
Distilled witch hazel	4 ounces

Use as a wash.

Perspiring Feet.

Salicylic acid	½ ounce
Powdered alum	½ "
Starch, finely powdered	½ "

Mix thoroughly and dust in the stockings every morning.

Perspiring Feet.

Starch powder	1 pound
Salicylic acid	2½ drachms

This mixture, which is best left unperfumed, does excellent service when used to prevent an offensive odor in stockings or shoes. The inside of the stockings is dusted with the powder and every week a teaspoonful is sprinkled into the shoes.

Perspiring Feet.

Solution chloride of iron	7½ drachms
Glycerine	2½ "
Oil bergamot	5 ounces

Mix. To be applied either with a camel's hair brush or a feather, on the soles and between the toes. A few treatments will effect a cure.

Perspiring Feet.

French chalk	40 parts
Subnitrate bismuth	45 "
Permanganate potash	13 "
Salicylate sodium	2 "

This powder should be dusted daily into the stockings. The feet should be washed every morning and evening, and after washing rubbed with alcohol.

Tender Feet.

Those who suffer from sore or tender feet after an unusually long walk, experience great relief from soaking the feet once or twice a week in a half pailful of hot water to which has been added a piece of saltpeter the size of a small walnut.

Perspiring Feet.

1. Wear low shoes, wool socks, and dust the feet over twice a day with iodol. They will soon be as hard, sweet and comfortable as one could wish.

2. Wash the feet at night with very hot water, put on white cotton socks and immerse the feet thus covered in methylated spirits poured into a basin. Wear the socks all night. They will soon dry in bed. During the evening wear cotton socks and felt slippers, and keep the socks constantly saturated with the spirit. In a week the cure will be completed.—*British Medical Journal.*

Powder for Perspiring Feet.

Powdered rice............................2 ounces
Bismuth subnitrate......................7 drachms
Potassium permanganate..............3   "
Powdered talc............................1½ "

Mix. To be dusted inside stockings.

Sweating of the Feet.

Salicylic acid............................6 grains
Arrowroot................................1 scruple
Powdered French chalk...............3 drachms

Mix. Dust the feet morning and evening.

Corn Cure.

One or two applications with a camel's hair pencil of a mixture of equal parts of glycerine and carbolic acid will take the pain entirely away.

Soft Corns.

For soft corns between the toes it is recommended to apply salicylic collodion, or better, the following:

Soft soap..................................4 drachms
Salicylic acid............................20 grains

Apply on a piece of lint every morning.

Liquid Corn Salve.

Salicylic acid............................20 grains
Fluid extract cannabis indica........1 drachm
Collodion.................................1 ounce

Mix. Apply with a camel's hair pencil twice a day for 3 days. Then soak the feet in warm water and pick the corns out with a knife or any sharp-pointed instrument.

Corn Salve.

Yellow wax	6 ounces
Venice turpentine	¾ ounce
Pure resin	2½ ounces
Salicylic acid	½ ounce
Balsam Peru	½ "
Vaseline	1 "

Melt over a water bath and stir until cool.

Corn Lotion.

Tincture iodine	⅓ ounce
Acetic acid	⅓ "
Glycerine	⅓ "
Tannic acid	30 grains

Mix.

Corn Remedy.

Salicylic acid	9 parts
Extract cannabis indica	1 part
Collodion	48 parts

Mix. Apply every night with a camel's hair brush. The root should be clean before it is applied and the mixture allowed to dry thoroughly before it comes in contact with the clothing.

Corn Plaster.

Salicylic acid	1 part
Burgundy pitch	1 "
Yellow wax	1 "

Mix over water bath.

Corn Plaster.

Resin	6 parts
Balsam fir	6 "

Mix over a water bath. As the mixture cools stir in 10 parts salicylic acid. This can be spread on cloth or leather, as when used the corn must not be rubbed with the shoe.

Frostbites.

Peppermint water ... 1 ounce
Diluted nitric acid ... 1 "

Mix. Use externally by painting the parts once and afterwards two times a day.

Chilblains.

Solution of perchloride of iron ... 2 ounces

Paint the parts affected with a camel's hair brush or a soft rag.

Chilblains.

Flexible collodion ... 2 ounces

Paint the part affected.

Chilblains.

White wine ... 4 ounces
Citrate iron and strychnine ... 3 drachms
Tincture wintergreen ... 1 drachm
Simple syrup enough to make ... 6 ounces

Mix. Take a teaspoonful after meals 3 times a day.

Chilblains.

Liniment of belladonna ... 2 drachms
Liniment of aconite ... 1 drachm
Carbolic acid ... 10 drops
Collodion ... 1 ounce

Mix. Apply to parts affected.

Chilblains.

Icthyol ... 1 drachm
Benzoated lard ... 7 drachms

Apply twice a day.

Cold Feet.

Crystals of sulphate of strychnine ... ½ grain
Muriated tincture of iron ... 3 drachms
Alcohol ... 2 "
Simple syrup to make ... 4 ounces

Mix. Take a teaspoonful three times a day before meals.

For the Nursery.

Infantile Colic.

Bicarbonate soda	8 grains
Oil anis	8 drops
Mucilage gum arabic	½ ounce
Peppermint water to make	2 ounces

Mix. Dose: Teaspoonful every half hour.

Colic of Infants.

For children whose digestion is greatly impaired, and subject to colic with a tendency to increase in severity, the following will be found valuable:

Chloroform	8 minims
Syrup Rhubarb	1 ounce

Mix. Dose: 10 to 15 drops, up to ½ teaspoonful, in a little water.

Summer Complaints.

Chloroform	½ drachm
Compound tincture cardamom seeds	3 drachms
Tincture capsicum	3 "
Syrup ginger to make	2 ounces

Mix. Dose: Teaspoonful every 3 hours, or less frequently.

In the cases of babies, look well to their cleanliness; give them a salt bath daily, without soap, and keep them cool. See that the teeth do not bother them; do not let them suck sugar tits, for this article sours on their stomachs and is often the cause of many gripes.

Infantile Convulsions.

Put the little patient in a warm bath, temperature 95 degrees, and in less than two minutes the spasm is gone and the convulsed limbs relaxed.

Children's Convulsions.

Bromide Potassium ... 16 grains
Water ... 4 ounces

Mix. A teaspoonful every quarter of an hour or half hour, according to the symptoms.

Worms in Children.

Santonin ... 4 grains
Powdered sugar of milk ... 1 scruple

Mix. Make 4 powders. Dose: 1 powder for a child four to twelve years of age.

Worm Syrup.

Fluid extract spigelia ... 5 ounces
Fluid extract senna ... 3 "
Oil anis ... 10 drops
Oil caraway ... 10 "
Simple syrup ... 8 ounces

Mix. Dose: Teaspoonful at intervals until purging commences.

Bronchitis in Children.

Tincture veratrum viride ... 15 drops
Syrup ipecac ... ½ ounce
Sweet spirits nitre ... ½ "

Mix. Dose: 15 drops every 3 hours, for a child one or two years old.

Bronchitis in Children.

In the acute stage, where some fever is present:

Tincture aconite ... 12 drops
Syrup ipecac ... ½ to 1 ounce
Liquor citrate potassium to make 3 ounces.

Mix. Dose: teaspoonful every three hours.

For the latter stages, when the fever has moderated:

Muriate ammonium ... 1 drachm
Fluid extract licorice ... ½ ounce
Water to make ... 3 ounces

Mix. Dose: one teaspoonful three times a day.

Measles.

Simple syrup............................ 2 ounces
Dover's powder....................... 10 grains
Distilled water......................... 2 ounces

Mix. Give one teaspoonful every four hours as directed.

Rickets.

Gum arabic............................. 3 drachms
Oil of sweet almonds............... 7½ "
Phosphorus .... ⅙ grain
Distilled water........................ 10½ drachms

Mix. Take a teaspoonful three times a day.

Whooping Cough.

Hydrate of chloral................... 1 drachm
Bromide potassium................. 2 drachms
Syrup of wild cherry bark........ 1 ounce
Water to make......................... 2 ounces

Mix. Give a teaspoonful every four to six hours for the cough.

Whooping Cough.

Aromatic elixir of licorice........ 2 ounces
Quinine................................... ½ drachm
Water to make......................... 4 ounces

Mix. Give a teaspoonful three or four times a day.

Whooping Cough.

Extract belladonna.................. 2 grains
Mucilage of gum arabic........... 4 ounces

20 to 30 drops every 3 hours.

Soothing Syrup.

Monobromate camphor........... 2 grains
Tincture hyoscyamus.............. U. S. P.
Syrup lactucarium................... 2 ounces

Mix. From half to a teaspoonful two or three times in 24 hours.

Whooping Cough.

Fluid extract of hyoscyamus .... 1 drachm
Orange flower water .. .. 8 ounces

Mix and give 1 tablespoonful every 3 hours for child of 12 years. Smaller child correspondingly smaller dose

Soothing Syrup for Children.

Treacle .... 1 pound
Water .... 1½ pints
Stronger tincture ginger .... ½ ounce
Oil cloves .... 20 drops
Oil sassafras .... 30 "
Oil caraway .... 5 "
Oil anis .... 10 "
Alcohol .... 5 ounces

Dissolve the oils in the alcohol, then add the treacle to the water and mix. Dose: ½ to 1 teaspoonful, as needed.

This syrup contains no opium or other narcotics, and is therefore absolutely harmless.

Wash for Sore Mouth in Children.

Muriate cocaine .... 1½ grains
Common salt .... 15 "
Glycerine .... 2½ drachms
Water .... 2½ "

Mix. Brush gums with camel's hair brush several times a day.

Thrush, or Child's Sore Mouth.

Chlorate potassium .... 40 grains
Tincture muriate iron .... 1 drachm
Simple syrup .... 6 drachms
Cinnamon water to make .... 2 ounces

Mix. Dose: Teaspoonful every two hours to child two years old.

Sore Mouth Nursing.

Aromatic tincture eupatorium .... 2 drachms
Fluid extract hydrastis (without
    alcohol) .... 2 drachms
Water to make .... 4 ounces

Mix. Give a teaspoonful every hour during the day.

Diphtheria.

Corrosive sublimate .... 1 grain
Tincture muriate iron .... ½ ounce
Glycerine .... 1 ounce
Essence pepsin .... 1½ ounces
Water to make .... 4 "

Mix. Dose : Teaspoonful every three hours.

Diphtheria.

Tincture muriate iron .... 2 drachms
Glycerine .... 4 "
Syrup ginger .... 10 "

Mix. Dose : Teaspoonful every two hours.
Give a sponge bath of warm apple vinegar every few hours.

Diphtheria.

Chlorate potassium .... 1 drachm
Listerine .... 1 ounce
Water to make .... 4 ounces

Mix. Dose as gargle every two hours.

Diarrhœa of Infants.

Aromatic syrup rhubarb .... 1 ounce
Paregoric .... ½ "
Compound tincture cardamom .... ½ "
Lime water .... 6 ounces

Mix. Dose : One teaspoonful often, to children under 1 and 2 years, afflicted with sour stomach attended with diarrhœa, vomiting, etc.

Infantile Diarrhœa.

Bismuth subnitrate .... 12 grains
Orange flower water .... 6 drachms
Syrup comfrey .... 1 drachm
Syrup quince .... 1 "

Mix. Dose: Teaspoonful as needed. Especially useful in dirrhœa which accompanies thrush.

Diarrhœa Mixture for Infants.

Paregoric	16 drops
Bismuth subnitrate	2 drachms
Syrup	2 "
Chalk mixture sufficient to make	2 ounces

Mix. Shake the bottle each time before using. Dose: A teaspoonful every 3 hours to an infant of one year, in purging and colic.

Diarrhœa of Children.

Phosphate soda	24 grains
Syrup ipecacuanha	4 drachms
Syrup rhubarb	1 ounce
Tincture nux vomica	8 drops
Essence peppermint	10 "
Hot water	1 ounce
Simple syrup	3 ounces

Dissolve the phosphate soda in the hot water and then add the other ingredients. Dose: From 1 to 2 teaspoonsfuls every 2 hours.

Constipation of Infants.

Podophyllin	1 grain
Alcohol	1½ drachms
Syrup of marshmallow	6 ounces

Mix. Dose: Dessertspoonful daily.

Infantile Constipation.

Calcined magnesia	
Powdered rhubarb	equal parts
Sugar of oil anis	

Mix. Administer a pinch three times a day in the constipation of children of one to two years old; if the infant is only some weeks old, use both the rhubarb and magnesia in less quantity.

[The sugar of oil anis is made by intimately mixing 1 drachm of oil anis with one ounce of powdered sugar.]

Painful Teething.

Cocaine hydrochlorate	1½ grains
Tincture conium	20 drops
Syrup	2 ounces

Constipation in Children.

Best manna	1 drachm
Carbonate magnesia	1 "
Fluid extract senna	3 drachms
Syrup ginger	1 ounce
Water to make	3 ounces

Mix. Dose: one or two teaspoonfuls three times a day for child of two years.

See also " Pleasant Laxative " under Cures for Common Complaints.

Infantile Constipation.

Bicarbonate sodium	1 drachm
Tincture nux vomica	6 drops
Tincture cardamon compound	2 drachms
Simple syrup	2 "
Chloroform water	½ ounce
Water	2 ounces

Mix. Dose: teaspoonful every six hours for infant.

Convulsions of Teething.

Chloral hydrate	15 grains
Bromide potassium	1 drachm
Simple syrup	5 drachms
Distilled water	2 ounces

Mix. Dose: Teaspoonful every 3 hours.

Teething Syrup.

Chloroform	10 drops
Tincture Spanish saffron	30 "
Strained honey	4 fl. drachms
Glycerine	1 fl. ounce

Apply to the gums of teething children.

Simple Fever.

Fluid extract aconite	16 drops
Liquor acetate ammonium	3½ ounces
Sweet spirits nitre	4 "

Mix. Dose: Teaspoonful every 2 hours to child 12 years old. Less in proportion if younger.

Quinsy Fever in Children.

Tincture of aconite _____ 5 drops
Distilled water _____ 4 ounces

Mix. A teaspoonful at intervals of fifteen to twenty minutes to abate fever.

Emetic in Croup.

As an emetic in croup use alum and molasses, made thick. Give one or two teaspoonfuls, followed by cold water.

Croup.

Syrup wild cherry _____ 2 ounces
Syrup senega _____ 1 drachm
Fluid extract jaborandi _____ 2 drachms

Mix. Dose: Teaspoonful every two or three hours.

Membranous Croup.

Tincture muriate iron _____ 1 drachm
Chlorate potassium _____ 1 "
Glycerine _____ 1 ounce
Ammonia water to make 4 ounces.

Mix. Dose: Teaspoonful every two hours for a child 4 years old. [Also useful in diphtheria.]

Chafing of Young Children.

Bismuth subnitrate _____ 1 drachm
Powdered gum arabic _____ 7 drachms

Mix, and apply after washing the parts with castile soap.

Ointment for Chafe.

Boric acid _____ 7 grains
Lanoline _____ 12 drachms
Vaseline _____ 3 "

This ointment is to be applied to the affected area, which is first cleansed by the use of a mild soap.

Food for Infants.

Cream _____ ½ ounce
Milk _____ 2 ounces
Sugar of milk _____ ½ drachm
Water _____ 1 ounce

Brandy with Egg.

In the rare cases where it is advisable to administer brandy to infants, the following mixture is advised.

Brandy	1 ounce
Cherry laurel water	5 drops
Yolk of 2 eggs	
Powdered sugar	6 drachms

Mix thoroughly. To be given in the course of a day, a small spoonful at a time.

Nursery Powder.

To cure severe chafing.

Gum camphor	¼ ounce
Carbolic acid	15 drops
Oxide of zinc	¾ ounce
English precipitated chalk	2 ounces
Oil of neroli	5 drops
Oil of rose	2 "

Rub the camphor to a fine powder in a mortar, using alcohol to reduce it, and mix the other components thoroughly. Sift through a bolting cloth of 100 meshes to the inch.

This powder is invaluable for healing raw and irritated surfaces and for curing sunburn. Mix (one part) with three parts vaseline or cold cream, it forms one of the most useful domestic remedies, in the way of a general healing salve, that can be suggested.

Infant Powder.

Powdered boric acid	1½ ounces
Carbolic acid	50 drops
Powdered French chalk	14½ ounces

Triturate the chalk with the carbolic acid gradually added; then add the boric acid and thoroughly mix.

Wetting the Bed.

This trouble, in children, may be frequently overcome by administering fluid extract of rhus aromatica 5 to 10 drops in milk two or three times a day.

Nursery Powder.

Powdered Fuller's earth	9	ounces
Powdered boric acid	1½	"
Powdered oxide zinc	3	"
Powdered starch	9	"
Powdered orris root	1½	"
Oil bergamot	2	drachms

Mix the powders thoroughly, add the oil, and pass through a fine sieve.

To Stop Over-Secretion of Milk.

Dissolve one-half ounce of camphor in 12 ounces of turpentine and apply to the breasts when desiring to stop the secretion of milk.

Fissures of the Nipples.

Balsam Peru	20	grains
Tincture arnica	20	"
Oil sweet almonds	5	drachms
Lime water	2½	"

Mix. Rub on the nipple each time after nursing.

Membranous Croup.

Calomel	2 grains
Bicarbonate sodium	24 "
Powdered ipecac	1 grain
Powdered pepsin	24 grains

Mix and divide into 12 powders. Dose: One powder every 2 hours.

Children Threatened with Croup.

Wine of ipecac	3 drachms
Syrup talc	5 "
Mucilage gum arabic	1 ounce

Mix. Dose: Small teaspoonful every hour or two.

Scarlet Fever.

Oil eucalyptus	16 drops
Syrup acacia	2 ounces

Shake well. Dose: Teaspoonful every 3 hours.

Croup.

Muriate of ammonia	12 grains
Carbonate of ammonia	8 "
Syrup gum arabic	½ ounce
Fluid extract eucalyptus	1½ drachms
Syrup wild cherry bark to make	2 ounces

Mix. Give a teaspoonful in milk or water every two, three or four hours.

Ointment for Use in Scarlet Fever.

Oil eucalyptus	10 drops
Prepared lard (or vaseline)	1 ounce

Mix. Apply night and morning.

Scarlet Fever.

Fluid extract lilly of the valley	10 drops
Antipyrine	15 grains
Simple syrup	2 ounces

Mix. Give a teaspoonful every hour for three hours to abate fever; give again in six or seven hours.

Scarlet Fever.

Glycerine	1 ounce
Salicylic acid	48 grains
Distilled water	1 ounce

Heat in water bath till the acid is dissolved. Dose: A teaspoonful four times a day for at least two days; diminish to three times then twice for three or four days.

This is to prevent scarlet fever after being exposed to it.

Infantile Eczema, "Milk Crust."

Calomel	10 grains
Oil chamomile	5 drops
Powdered arrow root	1 drachm
Ointment oxide zinc	1 ounce

Mix. Use locally.

Inflamed Breast.

Plaster of belladonna and poke root. Apply after cutting a hole for the nipple.

Infantile Eczema.

Calomel	20 grains
Carbolic acid	20 "
Oxide zinc ointment	½ ounce
Vaseline	½ "

Mix. Apply night and morning.

Sore Nipples.

Oil of sweet almonds	½ ounce
Tincture of arnica	½ drachm
Balsam of Peru	½ "
Lime water	½ ounce

Mix. Shake thoroughly. Paint the nipple with a camel's hair pencil or soft rag.

For Common Complaints.

Lung Fever.

Powdered opium	2 grains
Quinine	24 "

Mix. Put in 8 capsules. Take 2 every four hours.

Lung Consumption—Spitting.

Gallic acid	1½ drachms
Fluid extract ergot	3 "
Laudanum	2 "
Simple syrup	½ ounce
Water to make 2 ounces.	

Mix. Take a teaspoonful every two hours,

Lung Consumption—King's Evil.

Syrup hypophosphites comp (Fellows)	4 ounces
Compound syrup red clover	4 "

Mix. Two teaspoonfuls after meals.

Lung Consumption—Cough.

Iodide potassium .... 2 drachms
Tincture of henbane .... 1 ounce
Syrup of tolu .... 1 "
Syrup of wild cherry bark .... 1 "
Water to make 5 ounces.

Mix. Take a teaspoonful from three to six times a day as necessity may require.

Lung Consumption.—Night Sweats.

Extract of henbane .... 48 grains
Sulphate of zinc .... 12 "

Mix. Make 12 pills. Take 1 pill every night.

Painful Dyspepsia.

Bismuth subnitrate .... 2½ drachms
Carbonate magnesia .... 2½ "
Prepared chalk .... 2½ "
Phosphate lime .... 2½ "

Mix. Divide into 40 powders. Dose: One powder before each meal.

Flatulent Dyspepsia.

Powdered sulphur
Carbonate magnesia
Phosphate lime
Powdered charcoal
} equal parts

Mix. Dose: One teaspoonful in a glass of water during the attack.

Dyspepsia.

Tincture capsicum .... 16 drops
Tincture nux vomica .... 2 drachms
Tincture gentian compound .... 2 ounces

Mix. Dose: Teaspoonful in water three times a day.

Dyspepsia.

Tincture of Columbo .... 1 ounce
Water .... 3 ounces

Mix. A teaspoonful three times a day before eating.

Bloating, Due to Dyspepsia.

Oleoresin capsicum	10 drops
Pancreatin	20 grains
Powdered ginger	40 "
Powdered charcoal	40 "

Make into 20 pills. Dose: One pill three times a day before meals.

Dyspepsia—Waterbrash.

Subcarbonate bismuth..............2 drachms

Make twelve powders. One powder in a tablespoonful of water, or preferably milk, three times a day before meals.

Dyspepsia—Heartburn.

Aromatic spirits of ammonia	½ ounce
Tincture of gentian	½ "
Water to make	2 ounces

Mix. A teaspoonful one hour after eating.

Dyspepsia.—Distension of Stomach.

Powdered cayenne pepper	2 grains
Powdered rhubarb	12 "
Powdered ipecac	6 "
Powdered extract nux vomica	2 "

Mix. Make 12 pills. Dose: 1 pill before meals.

Headache.

Phenacetine ....40 grains

Make into 5 powders. Dose: One powder every 3 hours.

Sick Headache.

Bicarbonate soda	1 drachm
Bismuth subcarbonate	1 "
Powdered gum arabic	1 "
Aromatic spirits ammonia	2 drachms
Bromide ammonium	1½ "
Syrup ginger	3 "
Distilled water to make	8 ounces

Mix. Dose: Two tablespoonfuls in water. Repeat if necessary.

Headache.

Citrate caffeine	1	drachm
Bromide sodium	½	ounce
Antipyrine	2	drachms

Mix and divide into 20 powders. Dose: One powder in water as needed.

Sick Headache.

Aromatic liquor pepsin............3 ounces

Take one or two teaspoonfuls after each meal as required.

Nervous Headaches.

Fluid extract gurana	1	ounce
Hydrobromic acid	1	"

Mix. Take a teaspoonful in a tumbler half full of water. Repeat if necessary.

Headache.

Muriate of cocaine	1½	grains
Sodium Salicylate	4	"
Caffeine	4	"
Simple syrup	6	drachms
Water	2	ounces

Mix. Take ½ when attack begins and the remainder in half hour or longer.

Headache.

Phenacetine	2	grains
Caffeine citrate	1½	"
Powdered sugar of milk	4	"

Mix. Take at one time.

Headache.

Aromatic sprits of ammonis	3	drachms
Bromide potassium	2	"
Camphor water	6	ounces

Mix. Take a tablespoonful three times a day.

Constipation.

Cascara aromatic....................6 ounces

Dose: Take teaspoonful morning and night.

Pills for Constipation.

Extract henbane .... ½ drachm
Rochelle salt .... 1½ drachms
Compound extract coloclynth ...... 1 drachm
Extract aloes (socotrina) .... 1 "

Mix. Make into 30 pills. Dose: 1 or 2 pills at bedtime.

Habitual Constipation.

Fluid extract cascara sagrada ...... ½ ounce
Tincture nux vomica .... 5 drachms
Tincture belladonna .... 2 "
Glycerine to make .... 2 ounces

Mix. Dose: Teaspoonful three times daily.

Pleasant Mixture for Constipation.

Cream tartar .... 1 ounce
Glycerine .... ½ "
Confection senna .... 1 "
Extract dandelion .... 1 "

Mix. Dose: Teaspoonful or more at bedtime.

Constipation.

Powdered extract nux vomica ...... 6 grains
Powdered extract henbane .... 30 "
Powdered extract ipecac .... 6 "
Powdered extract socotrine aloes .... ½ drachm

Mix. Make into 60 pills. Take from 1 to 3 pills on going to bed.

Diarrhœa Mixture.

Tincture capsicum .... 1 drachm
Spirits peppermint .... 2 drachms
Tincture opium .... 3 "
Compound tincture catechu .... ½ ounce
Tincture kino .... ½ "
Tincture krameria .... ½ "
Spirits camphor .... ½ "
Water .... ½ "

Mix. Dose: one-half to one teaspoonful, repeated as needed.

Summer Complaint and Diarrhœa.

Compound tincture catechu .... 5 ounces
Spirits camphor .... 1 ounce
Dovers solution .... 2 ounces

Mix. 10 drops on sugar every hour or two.

Diarrhœa.

Subcarbonate of Bismuth .... ½ ounce
Tinct. Lavender .... 1 ounce
Carbolic acid, pure .... ½ drachm
Tincture rhubarb .... ½ ounce
McMunn's elixir of opium .... ½ "
Simple syrup to make .... 4 ounces

Mix. Shake well and take a teaspoonful every two, four or six hours as may be necessary.

Diarrhœa.—Chronic.

Subcarbonate of bismuth .... ½ ounce
Sulphate Morphia .... 1 grain

Mix. Make into 16 powders. One powder to be taken night and morning.

Dysentery.

White wax .... 1 scruple
Cocoa Butter .... 90 scruples
Vaseline .... 64 "
Morphine .... 6 "

Mix into 12 suppositories. Use one every four to six hours to relieve pain.

Diarrhœa.

Compound tincture catechu .... 1 ounce
Tincture rhubarb .... ½ ounce
McMunn's elixir of opium .... ½ ounce
Oil of sassafras .... 20 drops
Compound tincture lavender to make. 4 ounces

Mix. One teaspoonful at intervals of two, four or six hours as required.

Dysentery.

Powdered gum arabic	1 scruple
Powdered rosin	½ drachm
Powdered opium	1 scruple

Make into 25 pills. Take one pill every four hours until relieved.

Dysentery, when Epidemic.

Tincture rhubarb	½	ounce
Morphine	1	grain
Cinnamon Water to make	1	ounce

Mix. Take a teaspoonful every two hours until four doses are taken, then at longer intervals as may be necessary.

Diarrhœa.

Compound spirits lavender	4	ounces
Sugar	½	ounce
Camphor water to make	1	pint

Dose. A tablespoonful every hour.

Cholera or Diarrhœa Mixture.

Laudanum	1 ounce
Tincture of cayenne pepper	1 "
Tincture of rhubarb	1 "
Spirits of camphor	1 "
Essence peppermint	1 "

Mix. Dose: A teaspoonful, to be repeated not oftener than once in an hour.

Diarrhœa.

Tincture of rhubarb	2	drachms
Essence cinnamon	2	"
McMunn's elixir of opium	12	drops
Subnitrate of bismuth	16	grains
Carbolic acid (pure)	1	drop
Aromatic liquor pepsin	½	ounce
Glycerine to make	2	ounces

Mix. Give 1 teaspoonful every two, four or six hours as the case may require.

Cholera Mixture.

McMuun's elixir of opium	6 drachms
Fluid extract ipecac	2 "
Chloroform (pure)	2 "
Fluid extract valerian	5 "
Oil of peppermint	2 "
Sulphuric ether	8 "
Alcohol	3 "
Sherry wine (old) to make	½ pint

Mix. The dose for a grown person is from 25 to 30 drops.

Salve for Hemorrhoids.

Chrysarobin	1 drachm
Iodoform	20 grains
Extract belladonna	40 "
Vaseline	2 drachms

Mix.

Itching Piles.

Calomel	1 drachm
Lime water	8 ounces

Mix. Shake thoroughly and bathe the parts.

Piles.

Powdered galls	1 scruple
Iodide of lead	2 drachms
Extract of henbane	20 grains
Compound tincture iodine	20 drops
Butter of cocoa	2 drachms

Mix. Make into 20 suppositories. Use 1 night and morning after bathing in warm water. Replace the piles.

Dressing for Burns.

White lead thinned down with linseed oil will form the best possible application that can be made to a burn or scalded surface, however extensive or however raw. Soak layers of absorbent cotton in this solution and cover all the burned spots. The pain ceases at once and healing goes on immediately. When the dressing hardens, renew it. No other measures are needed.

Pile Ointment.

Powdered nut galls _____ 1 drachm
Benzoated lard _____ _____ 7 drachms

Mix. Anoint the parts, after bathing in warm water.

Cornmeal Poultice.

Cornmeal _____ 12 ounces
Boiling water _____ 2 pints

Mix together while water is boiling. Apply while still warm.

Charcoal Poultice.

Powdered charcoal _____ 1 ounce
Bread crumbs _____ 4 ounces
Flax seed meal _____ 3 "
Boiling water _____ 1 pint

Bread must be softened in water previous to mixing with flax seed meal. Stir constantly, then mix with charcoal and apply.

Soap and Bread Poultice.

Castile soap shaved finely _____ 2 ounces
White bread _____ 4 "
Brown sugar _____ 2 teaspoonfuls

Mix with little hot water thoroughly and apply.

Mustard Poultice.

Powdered mustard _____ 4 ounces
Whites of 4 eggs

Apply to parts affected. Guarantee that this plaster will not draw blisters.

Yeast Poultice.

Yeast _____ 6 ounces
Flour _____ 12 "
Water, (heated to 105 degrees) _____ 6 "

Mix the flour with water, add yeast, set near to fire until it raises and apply to parts affected.

Flaxseed Poultice.

Flaxseed .... 4 ounces
Boiling water 8   "

Mix thoroughly and apply.

Pills for Torpid Liver.

Extract henbane .... 10 grains
Aqueous extract aloes (socotrine) ... 20   "
Compound extract colocynth 20   "
Rochelle salts 30   "

Biliousness.

Sulphate sodium .... 1 ounce
Rochelle salts 1   "
Infusion cascarilla .... 8 ounces

Mix. Dose: 2 tablespoonfuls three times daily.

Bilious Colic.

Gum guaiac .... 1 ounce
Whisky .... ½ pint

Mix. Dose: One tablespoonful in water after each meal.

Biliousness.

Dilute nitro-muriatic acid .... 2 ounces.

Dose: 10 or 15 drops well diluted before each meal.

Burns.

Take equal parts linseed oil and lime water. Mix and shake thoroughly and apply to burnt parts. Keep thoroughly moist until pain is relieved which will be in a short while.

Burns.

Add to any quantity of water as much baking soda as it will possibly dissolve. Dip soft rags in this solution and apply to the burned surface.

Burns.

Lime water .... 8 ounces
Linseed oil 8   "

Mix. Shake thoroughly and apply by means of cotton batting to the burned surface.

Obstinate Constipation.

Rochelle salts ... 1 ounce
Fluid extract of senna ... 1 "
Aromatic syrup of rhubarb ... 2 ounces
Mint water to make ... 8 "

Mix. Tablespoonful morning and night.

Chronic Sore Throat.

Paregoric ... 1 drachm
Muriate of ammonia ... 1 "
Syrup of tolu ... ½ ounce
Syrup of senega ... ½ "
Wintergreen water to make ... 2 ounces

Mix. Give a teaspoonful four times a day.

Chronic Inflamation of the Tonsils.

Fluid extract of licorice root ... 1 ounce
Quinine ... 30 grains
Simple syrup ... 4 ounces

Mix. Take a teaspoonful three times a day before eating.

Tonsillitis (Quinzy Sore Throat.)

First give a saline purge, such as a dose of epsom salts (a heaping tablespoonful for an adult) or a Seidlitz powder, or a bottle of citrate of magnesia, then have this prescription filled:

Tincture aconite ... 30 drops
Fluid extract poke root ... 40 "
Syrup tolu to make ... 2 ounces

Mix. Dose: One teaspoonful every 3 hours.

Gargle for Quinzy.

Chlorate potassium ... 1 drachm
Chloride ammonium ... 3 drachms
Tincture chloride iron ... 2 "
Powdered alum ... 2 "
Water to make ... 4 ounces

Mix. Use as a gargle four or five times a day.

Chronic Sore Throat.

Compound syrup of red clover........4 ounces
Iodide of potassium ....1 drachm

Mix. Take a teaspoonful three times a day after eating.

Chronic Inflamation of the Tonsils.

Bromide of potassium................1 drachm
Muriated tincture of iron............2 drachms
Glycerine ....1 ounce

Mix. Apply once or twice a day to the tonsils.

Quinzy—Inflammation of the Tonsils.

Chlorate of potassium..............1 drachm
Muriated tincture of iron...........1 "
Glycerine enough to make..........1 ounce

Mix. Apply well down the throat with a soft rag securely fastened on a little stick.

Ulcerated Sore Throat.

Lunar costic......................80 grains
Water ....2 ounces

Camel's hair brush dipped and applied to raw spots once a day.

Sore Throat.

Glycerine ....1½ ounces
Muriated tincture of Iron...........1 drachm
Chlorate Potassium.................½ ounce
Water to make......................4 ounces

Mix. Gargle the throat three or four times a day.

Ministers' Sore Throat.

Tincture of cubebs..................1 ounce
Ammoniated tincture of guaiacum....1 "
Syrup of senega....................1 "
Simple syrup.......................1 "

Mix. A teaspoonful in rain or soft water three times a day

Ministers' Sore Throat.

Fluid extract yellow root (not alcoholic) ½ ounce
Bromide of potassium ½ "
Distilled water to make ½ pint

Mix. Gargle the throat with a tablespoonful night and morning.

Thrush.

Hyposulphite of sodium 2 grains
Water 2 ounces

Mix. Gently wash the baby's mouth twice a day with very soft linen rag which should be used but once.

Sore Mouth—Aptha.

Chlorate of potassium 75 grains
Water 2 ounces

Mix. A teaspoonful four times daily.

Sore Mouth—Canker.

Powdered alum 2 drachms
Powdered extract yellow root ½ ounce
White pond lilly root 2 drachms

Mix. Use dry on the affected part or put a half teaspoonful in a gill of boiling hot water, let stand half an hour and rinse the mouth.

Catarrh in the Head.

Take a clean napkin (folded) pour on the center of it about an ounce of spirits of camphor. Spread the napkin out and allow the alcohol to evaporate, refold and press the napkin over your mouth and nose and breathe through it for 15 or 20 minutes. You will be astonished at the relief obtained. Do this several times a day and it will effect a cure.

Catarrh.

Zinc sulphate 15 grains
Thymol ⅓ grain
Alcohol 1½ drachms
Glycerine 1½ "
Peppermint water 10 ounces

Mix. Use as a gargle and snuff up the nose.

Catarrh.

Glycerine	3 ounces
Carbolic acid (pure)	½ drachm
Powdered borax	2 drachms
Baking soda (best)	2 "
Distilled Water	1 quart

Mix. Use a wineglassful locally morning and night, after cleaning nose with warm water.

Catarrh—Chronic.

Iodide of lime	16 grains
Compound syrup of red clover	½ pint

Mix. A teaspoonful three times a day if scrofulous, or there is ulceration.

Cold in the Head.—Nasal Catarrh.

Tincture cayenne pepper	5 drops
Wine of ipecac	30 "
Laudanum	15 "
Water to make	1 ounce

Mix. Take at one dose on going to bed after a hot foot bath.

To Break A Cold.

Tincture aconite	1 drachm
Tincture belladona	2 drachms
Simple syrup	4 ounces

One teaspoonful every three hours.

A Snuff for Cold in the Head.

Menthol	6 grains
Powdered boric acid	2 drachms
Bismuth subnitrate	3 "
Powdered benzoin	3 "

Mix. A good sized pinch of this may be snuffed up 5 or 6 times a day. If the nose is very sensitive 1 grain of morphine may be added to the mixture.

A Good Iron Tonic.

Citrate iron and quinine............ 4 drachms
Citric acid........................40 grains
Tincture quassia................... 2 ounces
Glycerine .... 2 "
Chloroform........................ 1 ounce
Distilled water sufficient to make....12 ounces

Mix. Tablespoonful after meals.

A Good General Tonic.

Citrate iron and ammomia..........2 drachms
Tincture nux vomica...............1 drachm
Fluid extract orange peel.........1 "
Elixir calisaya...................½ ounce
Syrup, sufficient to make.........4 ounces

Teaspoonful after meals.

Tonic Bitters.

Red peruvian bark.................1 ounce
Gentian bruised...................½ ounce
Calombo bruised...................½ "
Elixir vitriol ....1 "
Port wine.........................1 quart

Mix. Two tablespoonfuls thrice daily.

Liniment for Bruises.

Tincture capsicum.................2 parts
Tincture myrrh....................1 part
Tincture opium....................2 parts
Tincture guaiac...................1 part
Spirits camphor...................8 parts

Mix. Use locally.

Liniment.

Tincture aconite..................⎫
Tincture opium....................⎬ equal parts.
Chloroform........................⎭

Mix. Shake well before using.

A Useful Liniment.

Oil origanum
Tincture opium
Spirits ammonia
Olive oil
} equal parts

Mix. Shake well before using. Apply with gentle friction.

In acute inflammation, in bruises or soreness, or stiffness of joints and muscles, this liniment will be found exceptionally serviceably. It should not be used on mucous surfaces nor where the skin is broken.

White's Liniment.

Vinegar .... 1 pint
Eggs .... three
Camphor .... 3 ounces
Turpentine .... 3 "

Beat eggs together smooth; add slowly vinegar first, camphor next and turpentine last, stirring all the time. Keep in well corked bottles. Shake thoroughly two or three times a day for three days, then it is ready for use.

This liniment is equally as well for beast as man. It will cure scratches on a horse, or sores, cuts, burns and other ailments in human. Cost very little.

Ointment of Tar.

Suet .... 1 ounce
Tar .... 1 "

Melt suet, mix the tar with it when at a moderate heat, strain while hot. Stir continually until cold. This ointment is for scabby eruptions, scald head. Should be applied morning and night. Keep the application constantly to the parts affected.

Liniment.

Tincture aconite root .... 1 ounce
Tincture arnica .... 1 "
Tincture cayenne pepper .... 1 "
Soap liniment .... 1 "
Chloroform .... 1 "
Oil of amber .... ¼ ounce

Mix.

Neuralgia.
Without Morphine.

Antipyrine	3 drachms
Caffeine	½ drachm
Extract cannabis indica	5½ grains
Extract aconite	5½ "
Hyoscine hydrobromate	⅓ grain

Make into 30 capsules, one to be taken every three to five hours.

Neuralgia.

Bromide ammonium	1 drachm
Salicylate sodium	1 "
Tincture henbane	2 drachms
Water to make	4 ounces

Mix. Dose: One teaspoonful every half hour until relief is obtained, or four doses have been taken.

Neuralgia.

Quinine	1 drachm
Sulphate morphine	1½ grains
Arsenic	1½ "
Extract aconite	15 "
Strychnine sulphate	1 grain

Make into 30 pills. Dose: One pill three times a day.

Neuralgia.

Methol	22 grains
Cocaine muriate	8 "
Chloral hydrate	5 "
Vaseline	2½ drachms

Mix. Apply to painful part and cover with court plaster.

Neuralgia.—Acute Nervous Pain.

Quinine	1 drachm
Pyrophosphate of iron	1 "
Sulphate of strychnine crystals	1 grain
Diluted phosphoric acid	2 ounces
Syrup of ginger	2 "

Mix. Take a teaspoonful three times a day.

Neuralgia.

Powdered extract aconite............... 2½ grains
Powdered extract indian hemp........ 2½ "
Phenacetine........................... 90 "
Caffeine............................... 15 "
Hydrobromate hyoscyamine........... ⅙ grain

Mix. Make 15 capsules. One as directed every one to three to five hours.

Neuralgia.

Morphia valerinate.................... 8 grains
Extract deadly nightshade............. 8 "
Iodide of arsenic...................... 1 grain
Powdered extract of gentian........... 5 grains
Fluid extract aconite root............. 5 drops

Mix. Make into 60 pills. Take two or three pills in the course of twenty-four hours.

Neuralgia.

Muriate of ammonia .... 30 grains
Camphor water........................ 1 ounce

Mix. Teaspoonful at a dose and repeat several times at intervals of five minutes if the pain be not relieved at once.

Treatment of Chronic Rheumatism.

Wear flannel next the skin; eat nourishing food; avoid undue exposure, especially damp weather. The following prescription is useful:

Bicarbonate potassium............... 15 grains
Iodide potassium..................... 3 "
Tincture henbane.................... 10 drops
Spirits chloroform................... 5 "
Infusion gentian..................... ½ ounce

Mix. To be taken at one dose three times a day.

Muscular Rheumatism.—Mumps.

Laudanum .... 4 drachms
Chloroform........................... 150 drops
Tincture of Aconite.................. 4 drachms
Compound camphor liniment to make 2 ounces.

Mix. Rub well on the affected part. Wear flannel underwear.

Chronic Rheumatism.

Wine of Colchicum root	1 drachm
Bicarbonate of potassium	3 drachms
Rochelle salts	3 "
Peppermint water	4 ounces

Take a tablespoonful three times a day.

Chronic Rheumatism.

Iodide of potassium	5 drachms
Tincture of guiac	2 "
Water	2 ounces

Take 1 teaspoonful four times a day.

Acute Articular Rheumatism.

Carbonate of Potassium	2½ drachms
Nitrate of potassium	2½ "
Water	8 ounces

Dissolve and take a tablespoonful three times a day.

Rheumatism.

Glycerine	1 ounce
Mucilage of gum arabic	2 ounces
Oil of wintergreen	180 drops
Water	1 ounce

Mix. Give 2 teaspoonfuls every three hours.

Articular Rheumatism—Acute.

Bicarbonate of soda	1 scruple
Calomel	5 grains
Powdered sugar of milk	1 scruple

Mix. Make 20 capsules. Give one every hour till the bowels move freely.

To Check Severe Nose-Bleed.

Dr. Jonathan Hutchison, the celebrated English physician, recommends plunging the feet and hands into water as hot as can be borne. He declares that the most rebellious cases have never resisted this mode of treatment.

Nose-Bleed.

Fluid extract witchhazel............... 2 ounces

Dose : Teaspoonful every one to three hours.

Nose-Bleed.

Sulphate of strychnia crystals .... ¼ grain
Muriated tincture of iron............ 3 drachms
Syrup of tolu, enough to make...... 4 ounces

Mix. Take a teaspoonful three times a day before eating.

Simple Colic.

Strong chloroform water........... 4 ounces
Decoction orange flowers........... 4 "
Tincture capsicum.................. 2 drachms

Mix. Dose : Teaspoonful as needed.

Painters' Colic.

Compound tincture cardamon....... ½ ounce
Tincture gentian compound.......... ½ "
Iodide of potassium................ 2½ drachms
Water to make...................... 4 ounces

Mix. A teaspoonful three times a day after eating.

Painters' Colic.

Tincture of aconite M. S. P......... 1 ounce
Chloroform......................... 1 "
Glycerine.......................... 1 "

Mix. Shake thoroughly before using. Saturate a woolen cloth and apply to the stomach, cover with a piece of oiled silk and hold in place with a bandage.

Colic of the Intestines.

Subnitrate of bismuth.............. 12 grains
Powdered pepsin, pure.............. 4 "
Morphine.......................... 1 grain

Mix. Make in 4 powders. Take 1 powder every thirty minutes to relieve pain.

Bronchitis.

Syrup tolu	1 ounce
Syrup wild cherry	1 "
Tincture henbane	1 "
Sweet spirits nitre	1 "
Water	1 "

Mix. Dose: Teaspoonful every three or four hours.

Bronchitis.

Muriate ammonia	1 drachm
Fluid extract licorice	½ ounce
Water to make	3 ounces

Mix. Dose: Teaspoonful three times a day.

Distressing Bronchial Cough.

Ammonia muriate	3 drachms
Morphir sulphate	3 grains
Spirits chloroform	1 ounce
Tincture squill	2 drachms
Syrup senega	1 ounce
Syrup of rock candy to make	4 ounces

Mix. Dose: 1 teaspoonful in water, every two or three hours.

Heartburn.

Carbolic acid	2 grains
Glycerine	1 ounce
Water	1 "

Mix. Dose: ½ to 1 teaspoonful in water before each meal.

Heartburn.

Baking soda (best)	320 grains
Aromatic spirits ammonia	60 drops
Peppermint water	1 pint

Dose: A teaspoonful. This preparation is known as soda mint.

Acidity of Stomach.

Bicarbonate soda	1 drachm
Powdered rhubarb	½ "
Essence peppermint	2 drachms
Water to make	4 ounces

Mix. Dose: Teaspoonful after meals.

Sick Stomach.

Beechwood creosote .... 4 drops
Lime water .... 2 ounces

Mix. Dose: Teaspoonful every fifteen minutes until stomach is quiet.

Sour Stomach.

Lime water .... 2 ounces
Cinnamon water .... 2 "

Mix. Dose: 1 or 2 teaspoonfuls in water as required.

"Wind on the Stomach."

Oleoresin capsicum .... 10 drops
Pancreatin .... 20 grains
Powdered ginger .... 40 "
Powdered wood charcoal .... 40 "

Make into 20 pills. Take 1 or 2 pills three times a day.

Indigestion, with Bloating.

Bismuth subnitrate .... 1 drachm
Bicarbonate sodium .... 2 drachms
Powdered sugar .... 2 "
Powdered gum arabic .... 2 "
Powdered ginger .... 2 "

Mix. Teaspoonful of the powder taken with a little water after eating.

Bloating.

Naphthol .... 1 drachm
Carbonate magnesia .... 1 "
Powdered charcoal .... 1 "
Essence Peppermint .... 2 drops

Mix Divide into 15 powders, and take one before each meal.

When bloating is accompanied with constipation, use the following:

Epsom salts .... 1 drachm
Flowers sulphur .... 1 "

Mix. Divide into 15 powders, and take one before each meal

When diarrhœa accompanies bloating :

    Bicarbonate soda.................. 30 grains
    Prepared chalk................... 15 "
    Powdered nux vomica.............. 3 "

Mix. Divide into 10 powders, and take one with each meal.

Vomiting.

Persistent vomiting is often permanently relieved by the application of a small blister over the pit of the stomach. A prepared mustard plaster will answer the same purpose.

Obstinate Vomiting.

A few spoonfuls of very hot water will often relieve obstinate vomiting after other remedies have been rejected.

Cough Mixture.

    Laudanum .... 1 ounce
    Compound tincture catechu....... 1 "
    Spririts camphor................ 1 "

Thirty drops at a dose in wine or whisky.

Cough Mixture.

    Carbonate of ammonia............ 320 grains
    Fluid extract senega............ ½ ounce
    Fluid extract squills........... ½ "
    Paregoric .... 3 ounces
    Water........................... 1½ "
    Syrup of tolu to make........... 1 pint

Dose : A teaspoonful.

Winter Cough.

    Compound syrup of white pine.... 4 ounces

A teaspoonful at a dose three to six times a day.

Troublesome Cough.

    Fluid extract yerba santa....... ½ ounce
    Fluid extract grindelia robusta. ½ "
    Syrup wild cherry............... 2 ounces

Mix. Dose : Teaspoonful every two or three hours.

Cough Syrup.

Compound syrup squill	½ ounce
Wine of tar	1 "
Syrup wild cherry	2½ ounces

Mix. Dose: Teaspoonful every three or four hours.

Lemon Cough Drops.

Granulated sugar	10 pounds
Brown sugar	4 "
Licorice paste	1 "
Cream tartar	½ ounce
Tincture capsicum	½ "
Oil anis	½ "
Water	2 quarts
Lemon flavoring.	

When the sugar has been melted in the water, bring the solution to a sharp boil, add the cream tartar and continue the boiling up to a strong crack degree. Pour the mass out on an oiled slab, spread the licorice on the sugar and add the flavoring, capsicum and anis. Work these thoroughly into the batch, then roll out and cut into shape desired.

Bronchial Cough Tablets.

Granulated sugar	8 pounds
Brown sugar	6 "
Glucose	2 "
Licorice paste	1½ "
Tartaric acid	1½ ounces
Paregoric	1 ounce
Tincture tolu	½ "
Oil anis	¼ "
Water	2 quarts

Dissolve the sugar in the water and bring to a sharp boil, stir in the glucose and continue to boil until the crack degree is reached. Pour the mass out on an oiled slab, spread the licorice paste on it, turn the edges of the sheet, add the acid and remaining ingredients. Work all thoroughly into the sugar, then roll out and cut into shape desired.

To Kill Body Lice. (Pediculi.)

Corrosive sublimate	1 part
Vinegar	500 parts

This application is said not only to kill the vermin, but also to remove the nits.

Mercurial ointment	1 part
Vaseline	2 parts

Oil bergamot sufficient. Mix. Use locally.
This ointment will kill body vermin without fail in one or two applications.

Ointment for Body Vermin.

Vaseline	6 drachms
Salicylic acid	45 grains
Balsam peru	30 "
Borax	15 "
Essence Bergamot	20 drops
Ethereal essence anis	5 "

Apply to the parts affected.

Sore Mouth.

Chloride zinc	3 grains
Diluted alcohol	8 ounces

Mix. Use as a mouth wash.

Fever Sores on Mouth and Lips.

Muriate cocaine	2 grains
Morphine	2 "
Borax	1½ drachms
Honey	1 drachm

Mix. A portion the size of a pea to be applied on cotton several times a day.

Dropsy.

Acetate potassium	6 drachms
Spirits juniper berries	1½ ounces
Infusion digitalis to make	4 "

Mix. Dose: Dessertspoonful every three hours.

Dropsy.

Infusion digitalis .... 4 ounces

Dose : Tablespoonful three times daily.

Impoverished Blood.

Carbonate of potassium (pure) ...... 2 drachms
Powdered Sulphate of iron .... 2 "
Powdered gum tragacanth sufficient quantity.

Mix. Make into 48 pills. Take 1 pill three times daily and an additional pill every three days until you take three pills three times a day.

Impoverished Blood.

Arseniate of sodium .... 3 grains
Corrosive sublimate .... 1 grain
Sulphate of strychnine .... ½ "
Bitter wine of iron .... 1 pint

Mix. Two teaspoonfuls in water after meals.

Involuntary Discharge of Urine.

Muriated tincture of iron .... 2 drachms
Elixir simple to make .... 4 ounces

Mix. Take a teaspoonful three times a day before eating.

Involuntary Discharge of Urine.

Mucilage of flaxseed .... 4 ounces
Calomel .... 4 grains

Mix. Shake well and inject half on going to bed and the remainder in the morning.

Involuntary Discharge of Urine.

Tincturd deadly nightshade made
  from English leaves .... 1 drachm
Elixir simple .... 2 ounces

Mix. Give a teasposnful three times a day two hours after eating.

Saint Vitus Dance.

Gourd seeds .... 1 ounce
Granulated sugar .... 10 drachms
Sweet milk .... 4 ounces

Make an emulsion by thoroughly incorporating the ingredients and strain through fine cloth. Take half early in the morning followed by a dose of castor oil two hours later. If there are worms then take the following prescription :

Fellows comp. syrup hypophosphites ½ pint

Take a teaspoonful three times a day for four or five weeks either before or after eating.

Blood in the Urine.

Fluid extract deadly nightshade ..... ½ drachm
Muriated tincture iron .... ½ ounce
Simple elixir to make .... 2 ounces

Mix. Give a teaspoonful every four hours.

Earache.

Glycerine .... 3 drachms
Chloral camphorated .... ½ drachm
Sweet almond oil .... 1 drachm

Mix. Apply to the ear on a piece of cotton, and rub before and behind the ear.

Earache.

Chloroform .... 1 part
Olive oil .... 8 parts

Mix. Put from 20 to 30 drops of this solution in the ear, closing it with cotton. When the earache is due to a boil near the external opening of the ear, an application of a solution of one part of menthol in twenty parts of oil of sweet almonds often brings quick relief.

Earache Drops.

Camphor chloral .... 5 drops
Glycerine .... 33 "
Almond oil .... 3 "

Mix. Three drops of this mixture on absorbent cotton to be placed in the ear twice daily.

Wax in the Ear.—Hardened.

Boracic acid .... 1 drachm
Glycerine .... 1½ ounces
Water .... 1½ "

Mix. Inject in ear once in twenty-four hours.

For Softening Ear Wax.

Boric acid	5 grains
Glycerine	1 ounce
Water	1 "

Warm this solution before using, and place 5 or 10 drops in the ear twice a day.

Asthma.

Chlorodine	2 drachms
Syrup of squills	1 ounce
Tincture of lobelia	½ "
Fluid extract of lily of the valley	1 drachm
Simple syrup	4 ounces

Mix. Take a teaspoonful every three hours or more frequently as may be required.

Asthma.

Compound asafoetida pill	½ drachm
Valerianate of zinc	15 grains

Mix. Make 15 pills. Dose: Take one three times a day, in the intervals a two grain quinine capsule.

Black Eye.

Mucilage gum arabic	1 drachm
Tincture cayenne pepper	1 "
Glycerine	10 drops

Mix. Paint the part with a camel's hair pencil, when dry renew two or three times. Do not let any get into the eyes.

Granulated Eyelids.

Yellow oxide mercury	4 grains
Simple cerate	2 drachms

Mix. Use locally twice daily.

Swolen Eyes.

If the eyes are swollen, use on them:

Boric acid	12 grains
Camphor water	2 ounces
Distilled water	2 "

Mix. Bathe and drop in the eyes frequently.

Weak Eyes.

Sulphate zinc............................. ½ grain
Powdered borax........................2 grains
Camphor water.........................2 drachms
Distilled water.........................2 "

Mix. 3 drops in each eye two or three times a day.

To Prevent Black Eye.

Take equal parts tincture cayenne pepper and mucilage of gum arabic to which add a few drops glycerine. This should be painted all over the bruised surface with a camel's hair pencil, and allowed to dry on, a second or third coating being applied as soon as the first is dry. If done as soon as the injury is inflicted, treatment will invariably prevent the blackening of the bruised tissues. The same remedy has no equal in rheumatic sore or stiff neck.

Eyewater.

Sulphate of zinc.........................1 grain
Sugar of lead.............................2 grains
Rose water................................1½ ounces
Vine of opium............................6 drops

Mix and filter. One drop in each eye night and morning.

Insomnia.—(Sleeplessness).

Bromide potassium.....................½ ounce
Chloral hydrate..........................2 drachms
Syrup wild cherry......................1 ounce
Water to make...........................3 ounces

Mix. Dose: Dessertspoonful in a wineglassful of water at bedtime.

Sleeplessness.

Bromide potassium.....................2 scruples
Chloral.....................................40 grains
Chocolate syrup.........................1 ounce
Gum arabic syrup......................½ "
Simple elixir.............................½ "

Mix. Take a tablespoonful about one quarter of an hour before going to bed.

Affections of the Liver.

Diluted nitro-muriatic acid ..... 3 drachms
Pure water to make .... 2 ounces

Mix. A teaspoonful before meals three times a day.

Affections of the Liver.—Functional.

Sulphate of sodium .... 1 ounce
Water enough to dissolve
Aromatic sulphuric acid .... 11 drops

Mix. Take ½ on going to bed, the remainder in the morning, if necessary to cause a free passage.

To Stimulate Appetite.

Dilute phosphoric acid .... ½ ounce
Dilute nitro-muriatic acid ...... ½ "
Aromatic sulphuric .... ½ "
Tincture chloride iron .... ½ "

Mix. Dose: 30 drops in ½ glass cold sweetened water during meals.

French (Raspail's) Enteric Bitters.

(Digestive, tonic, carnimative and anti-choleraic.)

Angelica root .... 7 drachms
Sweet flag root .... ½ drachm
Myrrh .... ½ "
Cinnamon .... ½ "
Aloes (socotrine) .... 15 grains
Cloves .... 15 "
Vanilla bean .... 15 "
Gum camphor .... 8 "
Nutmeg .... 4 "
Saffron .... 2 "
Alcohol (56 per cent.) .... 1 quart

Place in a tight-stoppered bottle, allow to digest in the sun several days, then filter through cloth and add a glass of good brandy.

Iron Tonic for Enriching the Blood, Etc.

Bitter wine of iron
Citrate of iron and quinine............128 grains
Simple syrup.......................... 4 ounces
Simple elixir to make................. 1 pint

Mix. Dose: A teaspoonful three times a day.

Epilepsy.

Tincture belladonna.................. 2 drops
Bromide sodium.......................15 grains
Chlorate hydrate..................... 5   "

Peppermint water to make one teaspoonful. Mix. One dose. Repeat as needed.

Epilepsy.

Tincture of gentian..................2   ounces
Bromide potassium...................2½ drachms
Distilled water to make.............. ½ pint

Mix. A tablespoonful twice a day for ten days, increase to four times for the same period then six times. Continue for a month.

Sun Cholera Mixture.

Tincture opium ....⎫
Tincture rhubarb.....................⎪
Tinctnre camphor....................⎬ equal parts
Tincture capsicum...................⎪
Spirits peppermint..................⎭

Dose: ½ to 1 teaspoonful every two or three hours when necessary.

Disease of the Heart Valvular.

Fluid extract lily of the valley........2 drachms
Simple syrup..........................6   "
Water enongh to make................2 ounces

Mix. A teaspoonful at intervals of four, six or eight hours as necessary.

Dropsy of the Peritoneum.

Cream of tartar......................80   grains
Powdered ginger..................... ½ drachm
Powdered jalap.......................2   scruples

Mix. Make into 4 powders. Take one every other night.

Canker Sore Mouth.

Tincture cayenne pepper	2	drachms
Tincture nux vomica	2	"
Quinine	30	grains
Tincture of rhubarb	½	ounce
Simple syrup to make	4	ounces

Mix. A teaspoonful three times a day before eating. As a local application use a piece of blue vitriol.

Salivation from Mercury.

Chlorate of potassium powder	3	drachms
Water	½	pint

Mix. Use as a mouth wash and take a tablespoonful every four or five hours.

Carbolic Salve.

Pure lard	4 ounces
Wax (yellow)	1 ounce

Melt wax moderate heat, add the lard gradually, stirring thoroughly together until cool then add 144 grains of carbolic acid. Mix thoroughly. This salve needs no recommendation. It is one of the best cures for healing all kinds of bruises, wounds, etc.

Resin Salve.

Resin	3½	ounces
Wax (yellow)	1½	"
Lard	5	"

Melt in a pan at a moderate heat. Strain through muslin or thin cloth. Let cool without stirring. This salve is a sure remedy for any blistered parts of the body, ulcers, chilblains, burns, etc.

Influenza.—LaGrippe.

Phenacetine	4 grain capsules.

Take one every four hours and two hours after a two grain quinine capsule.

Pleurisy.

Simple syrup	1 ounce
Divers powder	2 drachms
Water to make	2 ounces

Mix. Shake well and take a teaspoonful every two, three or four hours to abate pain.

Gout.

Wine of colchicum root	1 drachm
Magnesia	1 "
Peppermint water	4 ounces

Mix. 1 tablespoonful three times a day.

Peritonitis.

Elixir of opium (McMunn's)	6 drachms
Oil of turpentine	1 drachm
Mucilage of gum arabic	4 ounces

Mix. A teaspoonful every two hours.

To Stop Bleeding from Slight Wounds, Cuts in Shaving, Etc.

Mensell's solution ... 1 ounce

Paint with a camel's hair pencil.

Chronic Indigestion.

Spirits camphor	4 drachms
Bicarbonate of sodium	2 "
Compound spirits of lavender	2 ounces
Aromatic syrup of rhubarb	1 ounce
Peppermint water	8 ounces

Teaspoonful every half hour until relieved.

Tapeworm.

Croton oil	1 drop
Glycerine	10 drachms
Chloroform (pure)	10 "

Mix. Take ⅓ at intervals of two hours.

Bladder Irritation.

Tincture Hyoscyamus	1 ounce
Citrate of potassium	½ "
Fluid extract couchgrass	1 "
Fluid extract buchu	½ drachm
Water to make	3 ounces

Mix. Put a teaspoonful in a wineglass of water and take three times a day.

Typhoid Fever.

Nitrate of silver (crystals)............ 5 grains
Powdered sugar of milk... .... 30 "

Mix. Make 30 pills. Dose: Take one pill every four hours alternating with a one grain quinine capsule.

Sun Stroke.

Bromide of potassium................5½ drachms
Water................................. ½ pint

Mix. Give a tablespoonful every two hours for a week or so after consciousness is restored.

Delirium Tremens.

Chloral ....2½ drachms
Bromide of sodium..................5 "
Syrup gum arabic ....2 ounces
Chocolate syrup....................2 "
Simple elixir ....2 "
Distilled water to make.... .... ½ pint

Mix. Tablespoonful every 3 hours.

Gravel.

Syrup of chocolate....... ....1 ounce
Syrup of gum arabic................. ½ "
Chloral ....2 scruples
Simple elixir....................... ½ ounce

Mix. Tablespoonful every hour until relieved of pain.

Diabetes.

Phosphate potassium..................1 drachm
Water...............................5 ounces

Mix. Take from 1 to 2 teaspoonfuls three to six times a day.

Bright's Disease.—Acute.

Powdered ginger.....................40 grains
Powdered jalap..................... 1 scruple
Cream of tartar.................... ½ ounce

Mix. Make 8 powders. Take one every two hours.

Sore Eyes.

Sulphate of beberine _____ 1 grain
Distilled water _____ 1 ounce

Dissolve. Use as an eye wash.

Gastric Fever.

Morphine _____ 1 grain
Subcarbonate of bismuth _____ 1 drachm

Mix. Make 12 powders. Take one powder every three or four hours as required.

Sprains.

Opium and belladona plaster.

Apply to part affected.

Malaria.

Arsenic (pure) _____ 2 grains
Quinine _____ 50 "
Oil of black pepper _____ 25 drops
Oil of sassafras _____ 25 "
Sulphate strychnine (crystals) _____ 1 grain

Mix. Make 25 pills. Dose: 1 pill to be taken at meal time.

Carbuncle.

Carbolic acid _____ 12 grains
Iodine _____ 4 drachms
Glycerine _____ 1 ounce

Mix. Paint the parts affected morning and night.

Dropsy From Kidney Trouble

Powdered jalap _____ 1 drachm
Cream tartar _____ 6 drachms

Mix and divide into six powders. Dose: 1 powder every three hours.

Pleasant Laxative.

Confection senna _____ 2 ounces

Dose: ½ to one teaspoonful as needed. For children, ½ this quantity.

Lumbago.

Iodide potassium	3 drachms
Bromide potassium	3 "
Tincture colchicum seed	6 "
Syrup bitter orange peel	1½ ounces
Distilled water	3½ "

Mix. Take 3 or 4 teaspoonfuls in the course of a day. The dose is increased until some slight impression on the bowels is noticed.

Anemia.

Chloride ammonia	2 drachms
Tincture chloride iron	4 "
Glycerine	1 ounce
Water sufficient to make	3 ounces

Dissolve and mix. Dose: A teaspoonful after meals.

To Relieve Pain.

Spirits chloroform	3 drachms
Paregoric	6 "
Compound tincture cardamon to make	3 ounces

Mix. Dose 1 tablespoonful when needed.

This mixture is useful in spasmodic colic, cramps, convulsions, breast pangs, asthmatic paroxysms, etc.

Salve for the Cure of Excessive Sweating.

Ichthyol	1 drachm
Vaseline	1½ ounces

Mix. The application is to be made night and morning, the parts affected being washed with hot water.

Blackberry Cordial.

Blackberry juice	3 pints
Coarsely powdered cinnamon	2 ounces
Coarsely powdered cloves	½ ounce
Coarsely powdered nutmegs	½ "
Dilute alcohol	2 pints
Syrup	3 "

Pereolate the powdered spices with diluted alcohol to obtain two pints of tincture, and add this to the three pints of blackberry juice, then add 120 grains purified talcum, set the mixture aside for twelve hours, or longer, if convenient, occasionally shaking, then filter, and to the filtrate add the syrup.

Delirium Tremens.

Chloral hydrate	1½	drachms
Bromide potassium	2	"
Compound spirits ether	2	"
Tincture valerian	3	"
Water	6	ounces

Mix. Dose: Teaspoonful every two, three or four hours till quiet.

Muscular Spasm.

Tincture belladonna	½	ounce
Soap liniment	6	ounces

Mix. Use as a liniment.

Distressing Hawking and Spitting.

Take equal parts of ammonium chloride and powdered licorice, rub them well together- Take of the mixture a full teaspoonful in a glassful of water on an empty stomach in the morning, every two hours during the day, and the last dose before retiring. This is continued until one single attempt at clearing the throat will cause an easy and loose expectoration, when the frequency of the dose is reduced first to every three, then to every four, and finally five hours.

To Arrest Hiccough.

A dessertspoonful of vinegar taken pure, but with a little powdered sugar in it, will often arrest persistent hiccough, or ½ teaspoonful chloric ether in water.

HOUSEHOLD.

To Clean Marble.

Soft soap	¼ pound
Powdered whiting	¼ "
Salsoda	1 ounce

Blue vitriol size of a walnut.

Boil together for fifteen minutes and while hot rub it over the marble with a piece of flannel. Let it remain for twenty-four hours Wash off with clean water and polish with a piece of flannel or what is better, a piece of an old felt hat.

To remove Old Putty Out of Window Frames.

Paint the putty with a camel's hair pencil dipped in nitric or Muriatic acid. It soon becomes soft enough to remove with fingers.

Whitewash.

Slack a half bushel of lime in a clean, water tight barrel by pouring boiling hot water over it to the depth of five inches, stirring briskly. When slacked add it to the water, also 2 lbs. of sulphate of zinc and 1 lb. of common salt.

For a beautiful cream color add 3 lbs. of yellow ochre, pearl or lead color add lamp or ivory black in sufficient quantity. Fawn color add 4 lbs. umber, Turkish or American, one lb. of Indian red and 1 lb. common lamp black. For common stone color add 4 lbs. raw umber and 2 lbs. lampblack.

To Improve the Appearance of Oil Cloth.

Rub them with a mixture of half an ounce of beeswax in a saucer of turpentine. Warm them till they are thoroughly mixed and apply with a flannel cloth and rub with a dry flannel.

Transparent Cement for Mending Crockery Ware, Etc.

Gelatine	1 ounce
Acetic acid	2½ ounces

Dissolve by putting in a vessel and placing in boiling water.

Whitewash.—Government Reciept.

Lime	½ bushel
Common salt	1 peck
Ground rice	3 pounds
Spanish whiting powder	½ pound
Clear glue	1 "

Slack lime with boiling water, covering the vessel during the operation. Strain and add the salt previously dissolved in hot water. Boil the rice to a thin paste and add to the above, then add whiting in powder. Lastly dissolve the glue in warm water and mix all together. Let stand for several days. Keep in kettle in a portable furnace and apply to walls as hot as possible.

Black Varnish for Iron Stoves and Fire Places.

Stir ivory black into ordinary shellac varnish. Apply when article is perfectly cold.

To Clean Zinc Bath Tubs, Copper and Tin Utensils.

Wash them occasionally with a hot solution of vinegar and salt, then rinse them immediately in clear, hot water.

Ink Eraser.

Choloride of lime	¼ pound
Water	2 pints
Acetic acid	2½ ounces

Mix. Let stand for several days and filter through paper.

To Clean Marble or Tin.

Powdered oxalic acid	4 ounces
Baking soda	4 "
Powdered pumice stone	4 "
Sifted whiting	¼ pound

Mix well together. Moisten and rub on with a rag.

Furniture Polish.

Curd soap	4 parts
Spirits turpentine	5 "
Boiled linseed oil	5 "
Water	50 "

Mix.

Furniture Polish.

Alcohol	21 ounces
Linseed oil	14 "
Oxalic acid	1 ounce
Gum shellac	2 ounces
Gum benzoin	2 "
White rosin	2 "

Mix.

Furniture Polish.

Butter of antimony	½ ounce
Vinegar (best)	1 "
Alcohol	1 "
Linseed oil	¾ to 1 pint

Mix and shake thoroughly. Linseed oil should be added to make the mixture the consistency of cream. Apply with flannel rag, using plenty of friction.

Furniture Polish.

Wax	4 parts
Spirits turpentine	16 "
Linseed oil	16 "

Mix.

Furniture Polish.

Red.

Oil of turpentine	16 ounces
Alkanet	4 drachms
Beeswax	4 ounces

Digest the alkanet in the oil until sufficiently colored; then scrape the beeswax fine, and form a homogeneous mixture by digestion over a water bath. For a pale polish, omit the alkanet.

White.

White wax	1 pound
Solution of potash	1 "

Boil to proper consistency.

Furniture Polish.

Linseed oil	8 parts
Lac varnish	1 "

Mix.

Furniture Polish.

Linseed oil	2 parts
Shellac	3 "
Wood naphtha	8 "

Furniture Polish.

For Delicate Cabinet and Papier Mache Work.

Linseed oil	16 ounces
Alcohol	8 "
Vinegar	8 "
Butter of antimony	2 "
Oil of turpentine	8 "

Shake well before using, and apply with a wooden rubber.

Furniture Polish.

Oil of turpentine	8 ounces
Rectified oil of amber	8 "
Olive oil	8 "
Oil lavender	½ ounce
Tincture alkanet	2 drachms

Mix. A cotton rubber is saturated with this polish, which is thus applied to the wood. The latter is then well rubbed with soft dry cotton rags and wiped dry.

Polish for Fine Carved Wood.

Linseed oil	8 ounces
Old ale	8 "
White of one egg.	
Alcohol	1 ounce
Muriatic acid	1 "

Shake well before using. A little is to be applied to the face of a soft linen pad and lightly rubbed for a minute or two over the article to be restored, which must afterward be polished off with an old silk handkerchief. This will keep any length of time if well corked.

Floor Gloss or Polish.

Rosin	2 parts
Venice turpentine	1 part
Red shellac	4 parts
Strong alcohol	30

Polishing Silverware.

Use whiting and ammonia made into a paste and applied with soft rags, after wiping it off with a dry cloth. Some use a rag slightly moistened with vaseline, which has a tendency to prevent tarnishing of the silver surface.

Cockroach Poison.

A mixture of the following substances strewed around the places infested will drive away every one of the pests.

Naphtholine	2 parts
Powdered angelica root	300
Melilot	50
Oil eucalyptus	5

Mouse Poison.

Sulphate of strychnine	35 parts
Sugar of milk	35
Prussian blue	1 part
Common arsenic	70 parts
Wheat flour	300

Rub the sulphate of strychnine and sugar of milk together, add the Prussian blue and arsenic, finally the flour, and mix thoroughly.

Home-Made Fly Paper.

Common white arsenic, powdered	1½ ounces
Washing soda (sodium carbonate)	2
Boiling water	1 quart

Dissolve the arsenic and soda in the boiling water, and, while hot, soak in it sheets of coarse, unsized paper. After they are saturated drain and hang on lines to dry. Mark each sheet "poison." Glucose or sugar may be added to make it more attractive to the flies. It must be remembered that this paper will poison any animal life so it should be handled as any other poison. This paper will keep any length of time, as arsenic does not spoil.

To Destroy Fleas.

Place common sticky fly paper on the floor of the room infested, and in the center of each sheet a small piece of fresh meat. The fleas will jump toward the meat and adhere to the paper, and in this way even a badly infested house can be rid of the pests in a day or so.

Cement.

Make a solution of gum arabic and add plaster of paris to the consistency of cream. Paint edges with small brush and let dry.

Glue which will Resist the Action of Water.

Common glue _____ 1 pound
Skimmed milk _____ 2 quarts

Boil.

Adhesive Dextrine Mucilage.

A mixture of 10 drachms dextrine and ½ drachm glucose into which is dissolved a solution of 15 grains alum, 1 drachm glycerine and water sufficient to make 2 ounces.

Honey mixed in paste will cause labels to adhere to tin.

Liquid Glue.

Best glue _____ 120 parts
Acetic acid _____ 10 "
Water _____ 130 "
Alum _____ 1 part

Digest in water bath until dissolved, and when cold, add alcohol, 30 parts.

Liquid Glue.

Slacked lime _____ 40 parts
Sugar _____ 60 "
Water _____ 180 "
Glue _____ 60 "

Dissolve the lime and sugar in the water, heated to about 135° F., then add the glue, and after allowing to swell, again apply heat until dissolved.

Liquid Glue.

Glue	1 pound
Gum arabic	4 ounces
Glycerine	4 "
White sugar	4 "
Acetic acid	4 "

Dissolve the glue and gum arabic in hot water, add the other ingredients and enough hot water to make one gallon.

Liquid Glue.

Glue	1 ounce
Cider vinegar	2 ounces

Dissolve with the aid of heat.

Common and Good Disinfectant.

Commercial carbolic acid	7 ounces
Unslacked lime	2 "
Water	1 gallon

Mix.

Roach Exterminator.

Wheat flour	2 parts
Powdered sugar	4 "
Powdered borax	1 part
Unslacked lime	1 "

Mix and keep dry. Place around at night on pieces of paper.

Washing Liquor.

Slice 1 pound of white soap, stir it into 6 gallons of boiling water till dissolved, then add two ounces pearl ash, cool to a milk-warm temperature, and add 1 pint strong solution of ammonia.

Washing Powder.

Common washing soap	10 pounds
Caustic soda	5 "
Silicate of soda	3¾ "
Palm oil	½ pound
Water	2½ quarts

Mix together, filter and reduce to a coarse powder.

Javelle Water, for Washing and Bleaching White Goods.

Washing soda............................4 pounds
Hot water.................................1 gallon
Dissolve then add
Chloride of lime.........................1 pound

When cold strain. Keep in a well corked jug. A tablespoonful in a wash boiler half full of water.

Blueing.

Prussian blue............................1 ounce
Oxalic acid..............................½ "
Water....................................1 quart

Mix.

Liquid Bluing.

Soluble blue.............................2 drachms
Oxalic acid..............................½ drachm
Water....................................2 pints

Mix.

Liquid Starch Polish.

One ounce each of gum arabic and borax are dissolved in 10 ounces of water; 1 ounce each of white wax and spermaceti are melted, and while liquid are rubbed with the solution of borax and 10 drops oil of cloves to make emulsion, mixing them thoroughly. A teaspoonful of this mixture in a pint of starch gives a fine polish.

Magnesium Lemonade Powders.

Fine white sugar.........................2 pounds
Magnesium carbonate......................6 ounces
Citric acid..............................4 "
Essence of lemon.........................2 drachms

Rub the essence into the dry ingredients, work well together, sift and bottle.

Cream Soda Powder.

Fine sugar...............................30 parts
Tartaric acid............................7 "
Carbonate of soda........................6 "
Gum arabic finely powdered...............1 part
Vanilla flavoring, sufficient.

Thoroughly mix the ingredients, sift these through a fine sieve and cork tightly.

Baking Powder.—None Better.

Tartartic acid	10 ounces
Cream of Tartar (pure)	1 pound
Bicarbonate soda (best)	20 ounces
Powdered starch	2½ pounds

Mix very intimately.

Ink Extracts.

	PLAIN.	COPYING.
Tannin	1 ounce	9 drachms
Dried sulphate iron	3½ drachms	4 "
Gum arabic	75 grains	2 "
Sugar	40 "	75 grains
Aniline water-blue I. B.	40 "	75 "

The above quantities are intended for a wine-bottleful of rain water. The powder is to be added to the water, and the mixture gently boiled from 15 to 20 minutes, and when cold the ink should be bottled and set aside for four weeks before using.

Invisible Ink.

Onion juice or milk will develop a yellowish brown color on heating.

Invisible Ink.

Sulphuric acid	10 drops
Water	1 ounce

This ink, after drying is invisible, but when strongly heated it develops the writing in deep black characters.

Invisible Ink.

Linseed oil	1 part
Ammonia	20 parts
Water	100 "

Writing with this is invisible. Dip the paper in water and it appears and can be seen until the paper is dry, when it again disappears.

Grease on Wall Paper.

Cover the spot with blotting paper and press a heated flat iron over it several times; or, spray on benzine and proceed as above.

Cleaning Kid Gloves.

White soap .... 30 ounces
Water 21   "

Dissolve by heat, when cold add

Javelle water .... 20 ounces
Water of ammonia 2   "

Mix.

Dressing for Tan Shoes.

Four parts oil of turpentine to one part beeswax makes a fine dressing for tan shoes.

Lamps that Smoke.

The best means of preventing lamps from smoking is to saturate the wicks with strong vinegar and allow them to dry before using them. Following this little device one will be astonished to see how clear and brilliant a flame is produced by this very simple procedure.

To wash windows and mirrors add two or three spoonfuls of kerosene to a pail of water to be used for this purpose and the result will astonish you.

To Clean Plaster Casts.

In their natural state they are best freed from dust by covering them with a thick layer of starch, when the starch is dry brush thoroughly with a stiff brush.

To Save Coal.

Sprinkle salt liberally over the coal either in the bin or as it is put into the furnace. It will make it burn more evenly to a clean ash and will also prevent clinkers.

To Clean Light Summer Woolens, Etc.

Sprinkle powdered French chalk thickly over the soiled parts. Let remain two or three days and remove with a soft brush.

To pack dresses in a trunk lay newspapers smoothly inside the dresses that are folded and they will come out without creases.

To Clean and Bleach Straw Hats.

Sodium hyposulphite	10 parts
Glycerine	5 "
Alcohol	10 "
Water	75 "

Mix. Moisten a sponge in the solution, sponge the hat well with it, then put in a dark cool place for a day. Then go over the hat thoroughly with the following solution:

Alcohol	10 parts
Citric acid	2 "
Water	90 "

After again allowing the hat to remain for some time in a cool place, the hat is ironed.

Dandelion Beer.

Take one pound and a half of dandelion roots and boil them in two quarts of water for one hour, then strain and add to the liquid 20 grains of ground ginger, one pound brown sugar and one small cake of yeast; then one gallon and a half of cold water and put the mixture in a warm place to ferment for six hours. Then bottle and cork tightly and it will be ready for use in an hour or two. You should put the yeast in a little cold water and dissolve it before adding it to the ingredients.

Sparkling Spruce Beer.

Hops	1 ounce
Ground ginger	2 drachms
Water	1 gallon

Boil; when boiled, strain and add—

Molasses	1 pint
Essence spruce	½ "

When cold add a teacupful of yeast, put into a clean cask and cork tightly. Let it ferment for a few days and then bottle for use. If more convenient, the sprigs of spruce fir may be used instead of the essence.

Keeping Flowers.

Violets may be kept fresh if kept in fresh water and covered at night with a tumbler. Most flowers will retain their freshness for several days if kept over night in the open air.

Preserve Cut Flowers.

The flowers are cut early in the morning before the dew is off and are thoroughly wet by dipping into a solution of washing soda of a strength of about one ounce to one pint of water. After letting stand for a little time they are then dipped in a saturated wattery solution of salicylic acid, removed at once, and placed under a bell glass for a short time to dry.

Red Fire.

Nitrate of strontia _____8 ounces
Chlorate of potassia powdered_____4 "
Shellac in fine powder_____2 "
Lycopodium_____2 drachms

Powder separately, mix and sift.

Green Fire.

Powdered nitrate barium_____1 pound
Powdered chlorate of potassa_____1 ounce
Powdered gum shellac_____3 ounces
Powdered black antimony_____½ ounce

Mix.

Blue Fire, No. 1.

Tersulphuret antimony_____1 part
Sulphur_____2 parts
Nitre (dry)_____6 "

Blue Fire, No. 2.

Saltpetre_____8 parts
Sublimed sulphur_____4 "
Antimony_____1 part
Gum camphor_____½ "

Colored Fires.—(Poisonous.)

Blue.

Chlorate potash_____8 parts
Calomel_____4 "
Copper sulphate_____5 "
Shellac_____3 "

Green.

Barium nitrate	16 parts
Chlorate potash	16 "
Sulphur	5 "
Carbon	1 part

Purple.

Copper sulphide	8 parts
Calomel	7 "
Sulphur	2 "
Chlorate potash	16 "

www.ingramcontent.com/pod-product-compliance
Lightning Source LLC
Chambersburg PA
CBHW020137170426
43199CB00010B/786